DIRECTING YOUR
DESTINY

Hay House Titles of Related Interest

DIRECTING YOUR DESTINY

How to Become the Writer, Producer,
and Director of Your Dreams

JENNIFER GRACE

HAY HOUSE, INC.
Carlsbad, California • New York City
London • Sydney • Johannesburg
Vancouver • Hong Kong • New Delhi

Copyright © 2013 by Jennifer Grace

Published and distributed in the United States by: Hay House, Inc.: www.hayhouse .com® • *Published and distributed in Australia by:* Hay House Australia Pty. Ltd.: www .hayhouse.com.au • *Published and distributed in the United Kingdom by:* Hay House UK, Ltd.: www.hayhouse.co.uk • *Published and distributed in the Republic of South Africa by:* Hay House SA (Pty), Ltd.: www.hayhouse.co.za • *Distributed in Canada by:* Raincoast: www.raincoast.com • *Published in India by:* Hay House Publishers India: www.hayhouse.co.in

Cover design: Audrey Denson • Interior design: Pamela Homan
Interior photos/illustrations: Jennifer Grace

Library of Congress Cataloging-in-Publication Data

Grace, Jennifer.
  Directing your destiny : how to become the writer, producer, and director of your dreams / Jennifer Grace. -- 1st edition.
    pages cm
  ISBN 978-1-4019-4187-1 (tradepaper : alk. paper) 1. Motion picture authorship--Vocational guidance. 2. Motion pictures--Production and direction--Vocational guidance. 3. Independent films--Production and direction--Vocational guidance. I. Title.
  PN1996.G73 2013
  791.4302'3--dc23

                                    2013005831

Tradepaper ISBN: 978-1-4019-4187-1

16 15 14 13   4 3 2 1
1st edition, June 2013

Printed in the United States of America

I dedicate this book to my son, Cole, and his brother from another mother, Vince.

CONTENTS

FOREWORD

Many of you may not know who I am, but you certainly know my father, Dr. Wayne W. Dyer. Growing up in a home where my dad meditated every day and taught us how to be the powerful creators of our lives was such a rich experience for me. Over the years, I have been exposed to many amazing spiritual leaders and transformational teachers, so I know an authentic one when I see one. When I met Jennifer Grace and learned of her amazing tools that teach you how to feel the emotional truth of what you are trying to create by using acting methods, I knew I had stumbled onto something very different. I have seen firsthand how her step-by-step approach has worked for many people, and I have even used her program myself and was amazed at how effective it was. You are holding one of the simplest and clearest guides to manifesting your dreams, one that is truly unique. Jennifer Grace has been an incredible inspiration to me and to so many others.

I trust you will enjoy this book and its teachings as much as I have!

— **Serena Dyer**

INTRODUCTION

Flashback: I was 35 years old, my marriage had ended, and I proceeded to leave my career as an actress and filmmaker. After deciding that the life of a South Florida commercial actress was not fulfilling my soul, I embarked on myriad different entrepreneurial careers.

I started six companies. Along the way, I also drove my lawyer, accountant, ex-husband, mother, and best friend Audrey (who had to make six logos, one for each of my six ventures) absolutely crazy. I woke up each day and said to myself, *Today I am an actress! Now I am a photography manager! I'll become a spin instructor!* or *I'll start a nonprofit to combat cervical cancer!*

And so it went, again and again, for nearly two years.

By the time I was 37, I had no idea who I was, where I was going, or what I wanted to be when I grew up. I had wrapped myself up in false identities that I thought had been my life's purpose: wife, actress, filmmaker, nonprofit director, photography manager, fitness instructor, dance-company owner. But the only thing I had really become was a walking zombie.

Then a movie landed in my lap and introduced me to the Universal Law of Attraction. The movie revealed that each of our thoughts or feelings has its own frequency: negative or positive, productive or not. It also said that each of our thoughts and emotions is sent out to an invisible force field of energy and works like a magnet, attracting similar frequencies. If we have negative thoughts and feelings, the theory goes, we attract negative things into our lives. But by walking and thinking positively, and feeling positive at all times, we attract positive experiences.

That movie was called *The Secret*.

Like millions of Americans, and no doubt millions of Europeans, I watched *The Secret*—eight times, once by myself and seven times at vision-board parties.

We all went to those gatherings. Admit it—you did, too.

They were the parties where we all got out our chunky glue sticks and poster board and cut out photos of the fabulous places we wanted to visit. Then we cut out photos of dream cars we wanted to drive, drop-dead gorgeous models to marry, and dream jobs that would make us richer than Oprah.

Then we sat back on our couches and stared at our boards. We thought happy thoughts, just as the film had told us to do. The Law of Attraction, it had said, would manifest everything we desired if we just thought positively enough. And then, what happened after our many sessions of vision-board staring? What happened after we chanted, "Think happy thoughts!" over and over again for weeks and months on end?

Absolutely nothing.

Now, just because nothing happened after we popped a few blood vessels staring at pictures of sports cars doesn't mean that *The Secret* is a bad movie—far from it. For me, what the film did was crack open a door; it introduced me to the Law of Attraction. The trick was to then kick the door down. The film was an invitation, in fact, to seek more and find the tools to do the real work. Plus, the film led me to discover and experiment with two other universal laws: the Law of Attention and the Law of Action.

Because I watched *The Secret*, I gave myself an opportunity to uncover how this invisible force field of energy truly does connect us all and how I could communicate with that field through my thoughts, emotions, and beliefs. In my search to discover how to work in a practical way with this abundant energy field, three mentors appeared to me. All three arrived in my life at precisely the moment I needed them for my personal spiritual unfolding and professional understanding.

In the book you are now holding, I have assembled what I learned on this journey, added to it, and provided a structure that you will use to fulfill your destiny.

Getting Clear

When I was foundering in my attempts to find my purpose, I began seeing a therapist every week. I did this at the suggestion of my mother . . . and my ex-husband . . . and my best friend . . . and even my lawyer and accountant. Dr. Gurvit, my first mentor, quickly pointed out that I needed to change how I was approaching my life. It was time for me to stop the roller-coaster ride, wipe off the upper-lip sweat from running in circles seeking my life's purpose, and get some real clarity.

I quickly learned that in my desperation to "find myself," I had promptly lost myself. I realized that I had gone from one so-called passion to another without actually getting a sense of whether I was passionate about *any* of those endeavors. I hadn't allowed any time for introspection or discovery of what I really wanted. I hadn't created a life of happiness, but I had sure made one hot mess of myself.

Dr. Gurvit is not your run-of-the-mill psychologist. She is an advocate of meditation who turned me on to the joys and challenges of sitting with myself in utter silence. The work I did with her was simple yet profoundly transformational. She asked me to stop trying to find my life's purpose and commit to a serious three-month meditation practice.

During one of our first sessions, she brought in a glass of water, dumped sand and dirt into it, and stirred it up. She then said (referring to the dirt and sand), "These are your thoughts: your good thoughts, bad thoughts—your negative self-talk and your obsessive chatter that doesn't stop all day long. Now watch." She stopped stirring and let it all settle to the bottom of the glass. Then she instructed me to pick up the glass and look through it.

"Can you see though the glass now?" she asked.

I told her I could.

"That, my dear, is what happens when you meditate. All the thoughts that are stirred up get a chance to settle down. Then you see clearly."

"Aha!" I said aloud.

I love aha moments, don't you?

Inspired, I did the work. I meditated, I got more clarity, and I picked up the stones of my past and looked underneath them all. It wasn't always a pretty process. At times I had trouble just looking in the mirror. In the past, I would distract myself from my pain by working, socializing, or having a glass of wine. But now, I was facing the war that raged within me. If I was going to pick up the rug I had swept everything under and take a good, long look at all that had accumulated under it, I had to call upon courage.

In other words, I needed to become a spiritual warrior.

"Jennifer, warriors need courage to go into battle," Dr. Gurvit said. "It takes enormous courage to stop the roller-coaster ride you have been on and take a long look deep within. Know that being a spiritual warrior means acting with kindness, compassion, and gentleness toward yourself."

As I confronted myself about the failure of my marriage, I realized that I had chosen to be an actress because I was in need of constant approval and adoration. I came to understand that I had been easily swayed to do what others wanted and expected from me, because I lacked personal power and self-awareness. On June 22, 2006, near the end of my three months of daily meditation, something happened.

I was seated at my meditation station, about halfway through my daily practice, when everything suddenly felt different. I felt the entire world, all at once, moving through me. For one full minute, I felt absolutely nothing and everything simultaneously. I was present to everything in the room and intrinsically felt that I was a part of it. I was able to feel the energy of the plant in the corner, the pulse from the light streaming through the window, and the personality of the artist who created the painting on my wall.

My entire body exploded into an aliveness that I had never experienced before. There was no separation between me and anything else in the universe. I understood that I was limitless and a part of something that is always abundant and never lacking.

This was the energy field *The Secret* had spoken about.

When the chime on my meditation timer went off that day, I was surprised. My face was full of tears. During my entire meditation, though, I had not felt a single drop.

This experience became my introduction to the highest and best version of myself. Some of us identify this energy field as God; as a Higher Power; as the Universe; or, as has already been suggested, simply as an invisible field of energy. In this book, I will refer to this presence as Source. It is a presence that each of us has the potential to collaborate with and use to attain the sense of limitlessness that I experienced on that day in June. It is also what helped me to attract my destiny.

Shortly after that experience, my next teacher arrived with such divine timing that I knew Source was at work. Because I had taken time to get clear about who I was and what I wanted, Source divinely introduced my next mentor to me. As if on cue, Julia Romaine came back into my life.

My Life's Purpose Revealed

I had known Julia since I was ten years old, but we hadn't spoken for years. After she and my mom participated in the women's liberation movement together, they opened a women's center in 1981. My mom had been Julia's mentor. Now, almost 30 years later, Julia would become mine.

Julia called me one day, completely out of the blue, and offered to give me a ten-week Stanford University postgraduate class in transformation. She had become an executive coach and was certified to teach this amazing class.

Dr. Michael Ray had developed the course, Creativity in Business, almost 20 years earlier at Stanford. It was originally taught to business students to help them get in touch with their intuition, passions, and purpose. It consists of practical tools and experiential techniques designed to help students let go of their usual linear thinking and to tap into their essence as they find ways to think outside the box.

The course has been the subject of so much acclaim that it was cited as being one of the most life-changing classes ever taught at Stanford. After such sweet success, Dr. Ray decided it should be taken out of the classroom and into the world. That's where Julia came in.

Julia, who had been trained and certified by Dr. Ray, was teaching the course with Athena Katsaros, codeveloper of a version called

Creative Insight: Taking the Next Step. They presented it to over 400 women and men who had lost loved ones in the terrorist attacks of September 11, 2001. Representatives of The Bear Stearns Companies were so impressed by the idea that they awarded a $500,000 grant to Tuesday's Children so that the class could be made available at a minimal charge.

The individuals who participated in the course were asked to complete the same questionnaire before and after taking part. The survey was designed to measure happiness, confidence, and optimism about their future and goals.

The results were profound. According to the Creative Insight Report by The Bear Stearns Charitable Foundation, participants showed a 49 percent increase in personal growth and enrichment, a 48 percent more positive outlook, and an improvement in ability to handle stress by 44 percent. The majority of course graduates reported that the Creative Insight Journey had been a life-changing experience that had positively impacted their relationships with family and friends, made them more purposeful, and led to a greater commitment to their own goals.

This sounded exactly like what I needed, so I accepted Julia's offer of a "friends and family discount" and enrolled as her student.

Each week I learned lessons about dismantling my negative belief systems. I received empowering tools for transformation. I learned that I wasn't too old to find my life's purpose and that, yes, I could indeed reinvent myself at the age of 37. The course also gave me more clarity and insight about my life's purpose. During week five of the course, titled "Purpose and Vision," I reflected on how I had always been the person whom people had turned to when they needed motivation or inspiration. I had always been the cheerleader. After considering this and the goals of the Creative Insight Journey, I was certain that my life's purpose was to teach the course.

I was on fire. The veil had been lifted, and I knew exactly what I wanted to do. The moment I completed the Creative Insight Journey, I asked to be trained and certified.

After my training was complete, I was excited to begin sharing this course and to help others discover who they were, what their purposes were, and how they could use these simple and practical tools of transformation to cope with the challenges that all adults face: purpose and vision, time and stress, relationships, self-worth, prosperity, and work-life balance.

I was ready to launch my career as a Creative Insight Journey Instructor. By combining the eight years I had spent on Wall Street in investment banking with my creative world of acting, filmmaking, and screenwriting, I could perfectly blend my business knowledge and creative expertise to become what I called an "executive dream producer." "Business coach" and "life coach" were, after all, overused titles.

I also became more present to something else that I had missed back when I sat on the couch trying to think only happy thoughts and magically manifest my dream job, car, vacation, and lover. I realized that in order for Source to collaborate with me and help me to make my dreams come true, I had to *get off the couch.*

So I did.

I once again begged my friend Audrey to make one more logo. We created an incredible website, beautiful flyers, and a sassy new business card. I wrote a monthly newsletter, went to at least two or three networking events a week, blogged, and updated my social-media status with inspiring quotes twice a day, until I was blue in the face.

Then I gathered up all the amazing artists who had worked with me on my past failed entrepreneurial experiments and asked them to become my Dream Team. I assembled a business team to draw up a plan and a budget, a creative team to design stunning websites and brochures, and a marketing team to launch my clients' dreams into reality. My job was to keep everyone motivated, on track, and inspired! And then, with my business plan in place, my marketing machine ready to make my clients' dreams come true, and my couch wholly and consistently not sat upon, I hit a snag.

I still didn't have any clients—not even one. And, I was exhausted. I returned to my couch in the middle of my empty house, sat back down on it, and cried.

What went wrong? I had made a brand-new vision board, filled with lots of photos of a thriving business. I had the tools from the Stanford course to create a positive outlook. I had cultivated a relationship and was communicating with Source in my daily meditation practice. I had found clarity in what I wanted, and I was sure that I had found my life's purpose. I was definitely in action.

But still, no one had hired me.

You're such a loser, I told myself. *You will never succeed. Why don't you just get a job working at an office for a steady paycheck and stop trying to live your dream?*

Just before I was about to give up and go get that "real" job, Source delivered, in perfectly orchestrated timing, my third mentor: Christan.

The Movie of Your Life

For Christmas, my best friend Audrey gave me a teleseminar on quantum physics. It was all about how to use the basic principles of this amazing science to create the perfect life. The seminar's presenter, Christan, began to reveal some of the mysteries for me. I soon learned that quantum science has long supported the concept of manifestation through communication with Source. Christan introduced me to two authors with particularly influential work in this area: Lynne McTaggart, who wrote *Living the Field;* and Gregg Braden, who wrote *The Divine Matrix.* I had heard about quantum physics and had watched the movie *What the Bleep Do We Know!?,* but it seemed like a big ugly monster that would be far beyond my grasp. Nevertheless, this course helped me to clarify the often-complex scientific discoveries that had been made regarding Source.

Christan explained that, until the arrival of quantum physics, our society understood the world through the lens of Newtonian science. In Newton's material perspective of the world, the Universe is composed of discrete building blocks that are solid and unchangeable. Quantum physics, in contrast, views the world through a more spiritual lens in which there are no separate parts. Everything is fluid and always changing.

In Newtonian science, we are victims of our circumstances, and everything happens outside ourselves. We are powerless to control what happens in our lives. This is the embodiment of the expression, "You must accept the cards that life has dealt you." Quantum physics, on the other hand, teaches that we are the creators of our existence. Or, as Buddha said about 2,000 years ago, "With our thoughts, we make our world."

Finally, science and spirituality meet, I thought.

In the simplest of terms, the quantum findings show that everything we think, believe, and feel is channeled through our consciousness and that these thoughts, beliefs, and feelings manifest in the world around us. We create our own film, and this film is then projected onto a screen. It creates a holographic reality that we must then live in. So, in a sense, the inner speech, visual imagery, and everything else that comes from us is actually our life's movie. During those two years, every time I switched from one passion to another, I was trying to create a film titled *A Life of Purpose and Destiny.*

Instead it was called *One Hot Mess.*

Each of us can change and shape the energy of the world around us by becoming the director of our destiny. If you have found yourself starring in a movie to which you'd give two thumbs down, you can rewrite your movie by changing your consciousness. Part of this movie will be written, produced, and directed by you. The other part must be handed over, with complete trust and surrender, to Source.

When I was starring in *One Hot Mess,* I was not communicating with Source. I wasn't consciously writing, producing, or directing my story. Instead, I was sitting back and allowing life to happen to me. I wasn't mindfully getting clear about what I wanted. But once I began to actively manifest the life I wanted, I began to star in a new movie, titled *She's Got It Goin' On.* This movie was made possible by combining my intentions with action, my silence with surrender, and Christan was very instrumental in teaching me the art of surrender.

In my first quantum physics session with her, she told me I was *over*manifesting. I didn't even know there was such a thing. Apparently, I had decided that I would attract clients by attending networking meetings, writing a blog, and sending out a newsletter. Instead, she said that I needed to stop and do nothing. I needed to surrender and stop focusing on a particular outcome.

She suggested, "Wake up tomorrow, and go do what you love. Be open to your inner voice of wisdom and let it guide you throughout the day."

I felt as if I were back to square one. But I listened to her advice. I got up in the morning and decided that what I loved in that moment was an hour and a half of yoga. With all the driving and striving I'd been doing, I'd forgotten to take care of my body and spirit. So I got in the car and drove to a class.

On my way, a little voice inside my head told me to turn into Starbucks and get coffee.

But I don't have time for coffee, I argued with the little voice.

It would not relent. "Pull over, Jen. Go inside and get coffee—now."

Remembering Christan's advice, I went against the logical side of my mind that did not want to be late for class. I went into Starbucks.

A woman whose child went to the same school as my son was in line with me. We began to chat, and she asked me what I had been up to lately. I told her that I had been certified to teach a Stanford postgraduate class in creativity and business, and that I was now an executive dream producer. She lit right up.

"You mean that you executive produce people's dreams?"

I nodded.

"What fun! How do you do it?"

"I take an idea for a business that has been swirling around in someone's head and help that person realize it," I explained. "Along with my amazing dream team of experts, I do everything from helping people formulate their business plans and budgets to creating logos and websites. Then we launch their dreams into the world with a strategic marketing plan."

"Wow," she said and asked me for my card.

She wanted to launch a parent-coaching business. And she wanted to hire *me!* She was my very first client, although I didn't dare tell her that at the time.

The following week, she introduced me to two other people, and they hired me, too. I didn't meet them at a networking event, and they didn't find me through my blog or social media. They found me because I was on my way to yoga class and allowed Source to take over as I let go of attachment to an outcome. I just trusted.

That combination of being in action, while being in a state of allowing, is how I now guide my clients and students as they bring their dreams to fruition.

The Culmination

From that day forward, I began to direct my destiny and use the Universal Laws of Attention, Attraction, and Action to manifest the life of my dreams. I gained clarity and insight through learning about meditation from Dr. Gurvit, I used the tools that Julia had taught me during my training in the Stanford course to overcome limiting beliefs and get out of my own way, and I used the techniques available through the knowledge of quantum physics that I had learned from Christan.

Through my three mentors, I also cultivated my own system for communicating with Source. I designed a personal daily meditation and manifestation routine for my students and clients to create a life movie that they wanted to star in. I also uncovered my own secret formula to manifestation: to use the tools I learned as an actor to powerfully communicate authentic emotions to Source.

In this book, I will share this secret with you.

The personal-mastery work outlined in these pages is about moving from the audience to the director's chair. It's about taking your power back and coloring the movie of your life with imagination, vision, and truth. You will star in a film in which you get to be exactly who you are, comfortable in your own skin, and fully self-expressed in every aspect of your life.

Ever since I unfolded and deepened my ability to communicate with Source, I have enjoyed a continuous flow of abundance in all areas of my life. This abundance is a result of the practices I have developed and my firm belief that I am the writer, producer, and director of my destiny.

In this book, I'll share the components of what I've learned from these great mentors, as well as the groundbreaking method I have personally used over the years from being a screenwriter and actor. Everything is laid out in a simple, four-week, step-by-step program. It has helped me, and hundreds of my students, to create a life of peace, joy, love, and unlimited abundance. It is not a magic formula, but it is certainly magical. I hope this book finds you exactly at the point in your journey when you need it to arrive.

In fact, I'm sure it has.

How to Use This Book

This four-week program consists of nine practices organized into four parts. It will give you the tools you need in order to become the writer, producer, and director of your dreams. In Week I, you will learn what it means to be the writer of your dreams, in that you will acquire the awareness, clarity, and self-realization required to conceive of a movie that you would love to star in. To be able to manifest the life you want, you must pull everything you are thinking and believing into positive alignment; this is similar to how producers align the various aspects of a production to ensure a successful shoot, and it's why you will uncover what it means to be the producer of your dreams in Week II. But the way we communicate with Source is through the language of emotion; Source will only ever hear us through the genuine feelings that we experience. This is why I have given you the practice of cultivating truthful emotions—one of three practices for becoming the producer of your life—as the sole component of this program to be explored during Week III. And finally, in Week IV, you will learn how to be the director of your dreams by lifting them off the page and into the reality of the year's best movie.

I call these tools for transformation "practices," because they leave room for falling down and getting up again, which leads to growth and mastering something that matters. When we practice, we do not need to be perfect. I approach everything in life as if it were my practice.

I have a meditation practice, a writing practice, and a manifestation practice. When you step up to something with the idea that it's just practice, the critical voice inside of you that sends you negative self-judgments goes away and finds that seat in the audience that you just vacated.

Remember, no one ever picked up a guitar and became a rock star on the first day. As with playing an instrument, learning how to become the director of your dreams takes practice and a bit of daily discipline.

I have organized the practices into a simple, step-by-step system over the four-week program. Each week, you will participate in a series of exercises to build on what you learned the one before. By the end, you will have the tools for a daily 15-minute meditation and manifestation session, as well as additional tools for manifesting your destiny.

During Week I, you will spend approximately 10 minutes a day on these practices; during Week II, 12 minutes a day; and during Weeks III, IV, and beyond, a 15-minute routine to practice each day. If you can commit and be diligent with these practices every day for at least four weeks, they will give you direct access to the life of your dreams.

I suggest trying all of the exercises in sequential order. It is important to read each week's practices before implementing them. They are meant to work together. For example, you might read one week's worth of practices on Sunday evening and start your practices for that week on Monday morning. The Soulwork section after each week's practices will list your tasks and goals for each week.

I find enormous joy in my daily practices, and they are what I share with you in this program. And while I'm sure that you will find just as much joy in them as I have, there will be days when you really do not want to do them. Do them anyway. There is a light at the end of this four-week tunnel that will illuminate your future for years to come.

Now, I invite you into a world where make-believe can become reality, and movie magic actually exists.

Hurry up. The show is about to begin!

HOW TO BECOME THE WRITER OF YOUR DREAMS

Tools Needed for Week I:

✳ *A meditation station: A corner or room in your home for your daily practices. Set up either a chair or a small cushion on the floor. On a table next to it, place candles, flowers, and anything else that makes the space inviting.*

✳ *A journal.*

✳ *A great writing pen.*

You are a writer. In fact, everyone is. Your first step in directing your destiny is to say aloud, "I am a writer." Go ahead and do this now.

Whether we create a to-do list or a novel, we all write. We all tell stories, too. Even in the smallest daily activities, we tell stories. We use our creativity to paint the characters of our lives in order to make them interesting to the world around us. At our core, we are all artists.

Unfortunately, some of us were told early on that we weren't creative, and we believed that lie. Part of your work in this book is to stop believing those lies. Beginning today, you are the screenwriter of your life. You have permission to write the screenplay of your dreams.

When I was at a crossroads in my own life, I didn't take the time or space to discover the next best path for myself. I just began taking whatever opportunity happened to present itself to me. For example, when a photographer said I'd make a great agent, I listened to her instead of my intuition. I was in a state of desperation, and I began to take on other people's dreams. In short, I was blindly going along with my life when I should have been mindfully creating it.

Too many of us allow life to happen as it does, instead of shaping it as we want. We morph into whoever the person around us wants us to be. We are marching along to the beat of everyone else's drum.

Often, we are tempted to grasp at any opportunity that seems appealing, because we have not defined what we truly yearn for inside ourselves. But to navigate transformation—genuine transformation that's true to exactly who we are—we must become mindful and attain a clear sense of self. We must take time to be alone with our thoughts and feelings. We must dive into daily practices that help us gather insight, wisdom, and clarity.

The problem is, the act of reinventing ourselves and looking within can be scary—terrifying, even. In order to write the screenplay of our dreams, we must pay attention to our situation, be quiet, and seek answers to the hard questions: *Who am I? What do I really want?* Here, in this quiet place, without any distractions or people to keep us company, we are left only with our own thoughts. We're left with our insecurities and all of the little voices inside our heads that tell us that we're worthless and that we'll amount to nothing. So many of us are so terrified of this quiet place that we become completely paralyzed with fear and never even try to write a better screenplay than the one we're living.

But I've got a secret to tell you: people who are successful in life are just as afraid as anyone else. However, they don't let their fears paralyze them; they summon the courage to go after what they want despite those fears. In fact, fearlessness is not the absence of fear, but the presence of bravery. In order to move from my starring role in *One Hot Mess* to my far-better performance in *She's Got It Goin' On,* I had to put my pen of bravery to paper.

Your screenplay doesn't have to be perfect; it just needs to honor your truth. When you begin to live out what you have created, it will be a walking work of art.

And if you live it in the best possible way, it might just be a masterpiece.

Writing Your Movie

In the movie business, screenwriters must commit to an enormous amount of preparation before ever typing the first line of dialogue. They don't just start writing aimlessly. There is, for example, character research, when a screenwriter develops whatever it is that motivates and inspires the main characters. There's also the work of building a physical world where the characters will live, along with the development of their likes and dislikes, hopes and dreams.

To do this, screenwriters first observe and then take note of the world they live in. If they are capable, they make deliberate choices based on their research that then adds fluidity and direction to the film. I learned this process firsthand during my years as the head of my own independent film company.

Think about the movies you've seen on the big screen. They're undoubtedly based on a character who undergoes a significant trans-formation. That's called the *arc* of the character, and for a screen-writer to effectively write a story, he or she must first visualize the full transformation of the main character.

But, what about your movie? Like any good screenwriter, you also need to be crystal clear about the direction that your main charac-ter—you—will take long before you begin writing. Every so often, I hear from students who are just beginning one of my courses or workshops that they are trying to create the life of their dreams, but it just isn't working. Every time they say that, I ask them the first of two questions: "What *are* your dreams?"

"I have no clue," is what they usually say.

That's the problem. Most people are not clear about what they want. They have been hypnotized by what *other* people tell them they should want. A parent tells them that they should take over the family accounting firm. A friend tells them that they should settle down with a nice person and have kids. But they have no idea what *they* want. All of this uncertainty sends an uncertain message to Source. In turn, one lives in an uncertain movie. Perhaps someone has a job at that accounting firm she sort of likes, but feels that something is lacking. Or someone is in a relationship with that nice person who has *some* of the qualities he enjoys, but he still feels that something is missing. People settle for these experiences, even though there is some part of them way deep down that wants to write a different screenplay: *I like accounting, but I love making music. I like this person fine, but the sparks aren't flying.*

The second question I ask my students is, "Are you doing the first three practices diligently in order to find out who you are and

5

what you want?" Usually, they admit that they are not putting forth enough effort.

The practices I ask them about make up the first week of this program. And these practices also make all the difference in the world. They are:

※ *Mindfulness: Cultivating Awareness to Build Your Dreams*

※ *Meditation: Cultivating Clarity to Discover Your Dreams*

※ *Journaling: Cultivating Self-Awareness to Write Your Dreams*

These practices will become the foundation upon which you create the life of your dreams. They cannot be skipped over. There are no shortcuts to living a life you love. This work may not be the back-breaking work that kills people, but it does take a bit of effort to direct your destiny.

The Law of Attention

During Week I, we will explore practices and commit to working with the Universal Law of Attention. This law is the gateway between the conscious and subconscious minds. Its premise is simple: What you focus your attention on is what will manifest in your life.

It is important to ask yourself where your attention is focused. If you're always picturing whatever worst-case scenarios that you're afraid will happen, for example, you will attract the energy of those fears into your life. You are far more susceptible to experiencing those scenarios as a result.

The practices centered on the Law of Attention will help you to focus on both your outer world and your inner thoughts. As you learn to pay attention to positive things, your life will shift toward the reality you want to live. When you focus your attention on that positive side of life, you begin transforming your reality. This change is both powerful and magical.

Take a moment to revisit a time when you knew exactly what you wanted. Perhaps you really wanted to be on the varsity basketball team, or you heard about a college that offered the exact field of study you were interested in. That time surely had a different momentum than when you were unsure of what you wanted: you practiced drills every day, or you put everything you could into your college application. That is the Law of Attention. You became clear about what you wanted and took steps to make it happen. The clearer you are about what you want, the quicker that experience will come into the movie of your life.

Think of this program as laying down soil. During the next four weeks, you will plant seeds of intention within that soil. Each seed is a dream. You will learn to nurture the soil with clarity and awareness. When you plant your seeds, all you need is a little patience, and before you know it, your dreams will be growing. The daily practices you will begin during Week I will help you to get clear about your next steps so that this growing process can begin.

A Time for Listening

Becoming the writer of your life means being honest with yourself about what's working and what's not. It requires facing the truth about the job you're in, the relationship you're having, and the friends around you. Whenever I begin a workshop or course, I know that there will be at least one person who drops out. I can usually pick that individual on the first day, because he or she is too afraid to look into my eyes and isn't ready to face his or her truth. If the movie you are currently starring in lacks passion, purpose, and joy, then you understand from reading this book that something needs to be shifted and rewritten. You are not the person who will drop out.

Of course, it's easier to ignore a lack of passion and joy and continue sweeping all of your fears and doubts under the rug. But one day that lump under the rug will become so big that you can no longer walk around it, and you become unraveled. That's what many people call a "wake-up call." It's when someone is diagnosed with cancer, has a bad car accident, or loses a loved one unexpectedly. When these things happen, they shake us up and make us reevaluate our lives. We suddenly realize how precious, and short, life can be.

Instead, Week I will help you to begin inspecting the best way to lift up the rug and sweep the crap out from under it before life does it for you. It will teach you to slow down and listen. You will learn to come back to the present moment and tune in to what's in your heart. You will write down what your soul says to you and uncover your truth.

During Week I, you will need to set aside 15 minutes on a particular day to do the mindfulness practice, 10 minutes each day for the meditation practice, and 5 minutes daily for the journaling practice. Please read all three Week I practices, and then complete the Soulwork that's outlined at the end of Practice 3.

Practice 1

MINDFULNESS: CULTIVATING AWARENESS TO BUILD YOUR DREAMS

"The point of power is always in the present moment."

— LOUISE L. HAY

The first time I became aware of being completely in the present moment was during my first color walk. It was an assignment from my mentor, Julia Romaine, who instructed me to pick a color, walk out my front door (without a phone or any other distraction), and, for 15 minutes, look for the color I had chosen. I would see things, she assured me, that I had never noticed before.

I was highly doubtful. I had lived in my home for more than two years, and I took my dog, Max, out for two walks every day. How could there be anything I hadn't already seen? But I cast my doubts aside and chose the color yellow. Then I opened my front door.

The very first thing I saw was a huge tree with beautiful yellow blossoms. I gasped. My neighbor was standing outside her house. I turned and asked, "Did this tree bloom overnight?"

She looked at me rather strangely. "No, Jen," she said. "It has looked like that for at least three months now."

I was stunned. This beautiful tree had been greeting me every day as I left my house, yet I hadn't even noticed it.

Inspired by that eye-opening experience, I began walking the same streets that Max and I normally traveled. Yellow was everywhere: yellow benches, yellow birdhouses, and yellow doors that I had never consciously seen before. My eyes had physically looked at them, but only through the lens of the ordinary. Now that I was intentionally searching for this color, these items were there, clear as day and looking extraordinary.

What else have I been missing that has been right in front of my eyes all along? I wondered.

That's mindfulness. It's the act of being in touch with, and aware of, the present moment.

Source always gives us signs that will lead us to our intended destiny. Sometimes they arrive as amazing, serendipitous moments. Suddenly, the world is full of the details we need in order to move forward. Everything comes together in an instant, laying itself effortlessly at our feet. But other times—and frankly, far more often—our destiny is as hidden to us as the tree covered in yellow blossoms that we never noticed.

The Value of the Present Moment

Unless you're paying attention to the present moment, it's easy to miss what Source is trying to show you. In order for Source to guide you to the destiny you are co-authoring together, you must train yourself in mindful awareness. That's why this is the first practice in this book.

My life has been completely transformed by the practice of living in the present moment. I've learned how to let go of the past, for it is gone. I've learned how to no longer fear the future, for it has not yet been created. But when I used to read things in self-help books like, "Be in the present moment," or "Be in the now," I used to scream back, "I am in the present moment! I've been in the now since breakfast!" Then I began to realize what the great teachers who spoke those words were trying to teach me. I had seen it in my color walk, and this epiphany made me understand that personal transformation cannot come from merely reading a book. We need to put the book down and actually do the exercises. It is the only way to have a real experience.

I learned that going outside and communing with nature is particularly effective for grounding myself in the present moment. Others find it through walking in a park, going for a swim, or just sitting in their own backyards.

The physical locale that works best will be one that makes you more conscious and aware of your surroundings. When you find that place, you will suddenly realize that you are already living in the moment.

Living Outside of the Present Moment

Have you ever known people who are always worried about stuff going wrong? They constantly remind themselves and others about the negative things that have happened to them and the catastrophic events that they fear are on the horizon. If you pay close attention to these people, you will see their self-fulfilling prophecies start to come true. If they're always depressed about the poor relationships they attract, they'll continue to attract them. If they're afraid of going broke, they'll eventually go broke. The Law of Attention works that way: Where you put your attention is what you will attract.

You may also notice that these people are rarely in the present moment. Sometimes they're in the future, worrying about what may go wrong. Sometimes they even focus on scenarios that may never come to fruition. At other times, they're dwelling on the past. This is characterized by thoughts of regret about things that can't be changed—shoulda, woulda, coulda—and these mantras keep them focused on what has happened instead of on what their new reality can be.

It is true that reflecting on our lives can be helpful. Doing so can help us move forward. We also benefit from reflecting on what has or has not worked for us in the past. We can learn and grow from it. However, there is never a good time to worry or regret. When we worry, we experience fear and anxiety. When we feel regret, we also feel sadness, depression, or anger. If we spend our time mainly in our own heads, either in the future or the past, we cannot receive the universal signs that are being given to us. But we need to be aware of those warnings, because they point us to the destiny we are directing.

These signals come to us because of the idea I mentioned earlier, that we attract whatever it is we put our attention on. This is a fundamental concept of quantum physics, and it doesn't require a doctorate to understand or see. In the quantum realm, energy exists as electromagnetic waves that vibrate at different frequencies. There are higher frequencies, such as love, and lower frequencies, such as fear. Energy that vibrates at a certain frequency tends to attract frequencies of a similar vibration. In this way, energy has magnetic properties that draw similar energies together.

Think of Source's energy as a huge radio station in the sky that reaches us through whatever frequency we're on. It's as if it has a satellite orbiting in space. If your frequency is tuned to the station of fear and anxiety, or if it's tuned to the station of past regrets, you will receive that frequency. Fear attracts more fear, anger attracts more anger. When we dwell unhelpfully on the past or create fearful and anxious scenarios about the future, we get ourselves into trouble. But by training ourselves in mindfulness, we turn trouble into happiness.

My student Peter, for example, was still feeling a lot of pain three years after separating from his wife. He developed insomnia and spent every night regretting his mistakes in the relationship and worrying that he would lead a lonely life. When I asked him how he felt, he just said, "Sad."

I asked Peter to detach himself from his thoughts of what he could have done differently. I suggested that he, instead, just sit for a moment in the room and let go of those pangs of regret and reflection.

"Just stop and look around the room," I said. It had beautiful wood floors, candles, and soft-yellow paint on the walls.

He looked around and then looked back at me.

"I actually feel okay," he said. "I feel safe."

"There is nothing to regret or worry about in this particular moment," I reassured him. "All is well at this very instant."

"Yes," he said, smiling for the first time.

I gave him a thin blue string and told him to tie it around his wrist. The string would remind him to keep coming back to the present moment, where peace was available to him.

Just then, my student Betty knocked on the door. I told her that I'd be with her in a few moments.

"No, it's okay," Peter said. "She can come in. I'm all set."

I watched a little spark ignite between them as Betty entered the room, so I decided to follow my intuition and excuse myself for a moment.

When I returned, they were deep in conversation, both laughing and smiling. If Peter had not come home to the present moment just a few minutes before, he may never have noticed the gift Source had sent him.

I am happy to report that Betty and Peter are now in love!

By training yourself in mindfulness, you will learn to recognize which frequency you are tuned in to. Begin the practice of checking in by asking yourself, *Where is my mind right now?* Do this three times each day, and you will be able to recognize when you are in a low-frequency state. Then, gently tune in to the present moment and the frequency of peace.

We can only "be here now" by being in the present and looking for the signs that will lead us in the direction of our best possible future.

That's why it is so vital, when we're creating the life of our dreams, to stay mindful of tuning our attention and power to high-frequency emotional states like peace, joy, and gratitude. (I will teach you how to shift your emotional state using acting techniques a bit later, in Practice 6.)

Story Data

Screenwriters are trained to observe the world around them and collect *story data* for their characters. They learn to use the people and situations around them as tools to fuel the ideas behind their work. A character in one of my own screenplays was a wealthy woman. To prepare her story, I would drive through neighborhoods with mansions. I would also dress up and go into expensive stores to notice how salespeople treated me while I was in character.

Another benefit of being here now is in understanding that the world around you provides much of what you need for the movie of your life. As writers of our own screenplays, we need to do the same in order to experience what it feels like to be surrounded by what we wish for. Simply put, we cannot write the story of our new lives if we have no experience living in the world we strive to inhabit.

I recently did an exercise that allowed me to be in a different world while visiting my colleague, Pamela Jones. Pamela is an accomplished photographer who has a home in the South of France. While I was visiting, she happened to be bidding to photograph a $20 million yacht, and she brought me along with her.

I was starving when we arrived, and told her that I'd meet her on board after I grabbed food at port. Pamela went onto the yacht ahead of me and left my name with a crew member who would let me on after my lunch.

When I arrived 20 minutes later, a crew member was waiting at the velvet rope for me.

"Miss Grace?"

"Yes," I said.

"They are waiting for you upstairs, Miss Grace. Please follow me."

I decided to slip into the character of my future self and act *as if* this luxurious yacht were my own. As I followed the crew member, I began to walk taller and feel like royalty. When I reached Pamela on the upper deck, another crew member handed me, as if on cue, a glass of champagne.

"For you, Miss Grace."

I could barely resist saying, "Why, thank you, sir! Now if you wouldn't mind, please go run my bath!"

For that entire meeting, I sat on one of the comfortable couches overlooking Monte Carlo, playing my part. I was in character the entire time, even thinking the thoughts I would have if I were the owner of the yacht.

I had so much fun playing the role that when it was time to leave, it felt strange to go.

Later, I used Photoshop to place the words "Lady Grace" on a photo of a beautiful sailboat and put the photo on my vision board. I had never thought about owning a boat before, but that experience presented something to me that I believe will bring me joy. In fact, in the future-life script that I've written for myself (and that you'll learn to write later in this book), Lady Grace is mine. I know Source heard my call onboard the yacht that day, because I was so in tune with my future reality. Therefore, Source shall deliver Lady Grace to me when it is divinely timed.

There are stories to inspire us everywhere if we just pay attention.

One of my most dedicated students named Colleen, a jewelry designer, always dreamed of having her collection sold by Neiman Marcus. Once a week, she walked into the store and looked through the glass at other designers' jewelry. Then, she imagined her work on display there.

After that, she focused her power and attention on this dream every day during her meditation. Soon, Source delivered a synchronistic meeting with a woman who happened to know the chief jewelry buyer for Neiman Marcus.

Coincidence? I think not.

As I was writing this book, Colleen called. She had booked a meeting with Neiman Marcus! Her dream store was interested in carrying her line.

My student Debbie used the same technique to attract the perfect love relationship. She noticed that her friend David was very romantic. He was constantly sending his girlfriend flowers, opening doors for her, and telling her that she was beautiful. Debbie noted that she wanted a partner like that. She also collected story data from Max, her best friend's husband. Max was well traveled and adventurous. He fell short on romance, but Debbie knew she could manifest a man who was like David—present, kind, and romantic—*and* had the qualities Max used to live an exciting and adventurous life. He would be the perfect guy!

Well, the next man who walked into her life had all the qualities of the two men she admired and had collected story data about. Her first meeting with him was identical to the future-life script she had written. She knew Source had heard her call.

Another coincidence? I think not.

Creating a Mindfulness Practice

Our brains are like real estate. We have the space to build our dreams, but if that space is crowded with worry and regret, it's impossible to find room for the creativity needed to realize the life of our dreams. Mindfulness saves us from the negative chatter in our minds. The present moment is quiet and peaceful. When you have peace and quiet in your "space," you are clear to create.

By practicing mindfulness, we can better navigate even some of the most traumatic moments in our lives. For example, when my dad told me his cancer was back, I had a four-day wait to learn whether or not the diagnosis was terminal. In cases where we have to endure excruciating moments and don't know what the future holds, we often begin thinking of worst-case scenarios.

I could have allowed my mind to obsessively worry about my father's mortality for four days. Instead, I brought myself back to the present moment, where my father was still alive. I created space in my mind, free of worry and fear, by spending time in my backyard listening to birds and smelling the flowers that were in full bloom. That way, I could come back to the present and be an attentive mother, a focused teacher, and a positive daughter.

I call this practice the *Five-Senses Check-In.*

I've noticed that it's almost impossible to concentrate on a sense and a thought at the same time. If you smell a flower, it seems that you cannot simultaneously think about enjoying the smell. So if you concentrate on all five senses—smell, sight, taste, touch, and sound—you cannot concentrate on any disturbing thoughts you may be thinking.

Below, I describe the Five-Senses Check-In exercise plus several others of varying natures and degrees of difficulty. You can use each of them to help you develop your practice of mindfulness and improve your ability to live in a frequency that resonates with Source.

Exercise: The Five-Senses Check-In

I use the Five-Senses Check-In every day. You can use it before the manifestation/meditation routine (which I will introduce to you at the end of these first three practices) to clear your mind before you communicate with Source.

You can also use this exercise when you are trying to fall asleep, to erase thoughts that are racing through your mind. Instead of being distracted by those thoughts, you can concentrate on how the sheets smell or how the pillow feels.

The Five-Senses Check-In is a very simple exercise that you can use anytime, anywhere. It is guaranteed to take you out of your head and back into the present moment.

Now, stop reading for a moment and look around you.

First, concentrate on sight. Look at the colors and textures around you that you may not have noticed before. If thoughts about the future or past come to mind, simply shift your gaze to the next object.

Next, concentrate on smell. Breathe in the air and notice scents in the room. Open the window and let in fresh air.

Then, focus on sound. Notice any sounds inside the room, and then outside of it.

Now practice touch. Feel your clothing, the air on your cheek, or the way the sun warms your back if you're near a window.

Finally, taste. Run your tongue along your teeth, and swallow. Notice the way your mouth tastes. Is it stale or sweet?

With all five senses engaged at once, begin to notice your breath. Watch how it moves through your body. Finally, just be in the room. Understand that you are one with every living and nonliving thing around you.

Stay there for a few moments. Feel the deep state of peace you have just created.

You can do this practice throughout the day. It will bring you back when you are falling into a state of fear, anxiety, or scarcity. You will be aware of the unlimited creative energy field that is all around you, and you will be returned to a grounded state of centeredness and peace.

From this place, we can powerfully set the tone to manifest whatever we want.

Exercise: Where Is My Mind?

Another simple exercise that I teach my Creative Insight Journey students, and use myself, is checking where my mind is throughout the day. All it takes for you is a reminder on your cell phone that chimes three times each day.

When the alert sounds, take a moment to ask where your mind is.

Program your phone now to notify you three times each day.

When the reminder goes off, if you realize that you are not in the best place, bring yourself back to the present moment through the power of your breath.

Breathe in three times and say to yourself: *Be. Here. Now.*

Do this practice three times each day during Week I.

Exercise: 15-Minute Mindfulness

A more-advanced mindfulness exercise requires 15 minutes of uninterrupted time. Try this exercise once this week to deepen awareness and experience the present moment.

First, choose an activity that you enjoy doing. Then, set a timer for 15 minutes. Make sure your phone, TV, and computers are all turned off.

During this time, focus on your chosen activity with all five senses activated. Each time a thought about the future or the past comes in, notice it, let it go, and return to your activity.

During Week I, do one 15-minute mindfulness exercise. You can pick any activity that brings you joy, or try one of these:

- ※ **Cook a meal** with complete focus and concentration. If you are making a soup, notice how your arm muscles feel as you chop a carrot. Listen to the sound when your knife hits the cutting board.

- ※ **Take a color walk** by choosing one color before you leave home and then only looking for that color on your walk.

- ※ **Take a shower,** and feel the water and the way it drips down your body. Smell the soap; breathe in its freshness. Massage sesame oil on your hands and feet, and study your body.

🌟 **Eat a meal** in silence and taste each ingredient. Think about where each one originated, who grew it, and who drove the truck to the supermarket. Be mindful of the interconnectedness of it all.

The greatest benefit of mindfulness training is becoming more aware of your thoughts and emotions. The language of Source is one of feeling, and tuning in to your own feelings causes you to be more aware of the messages you're sending. When you catch yourself in a negative thought pattern, in which you worry about the future or regret the past, you can learn to quickly identify these negative emotions.

When you do this, stop and come home to the present moment. In doing so, you can send a more powerful message to Source, which, in turn, will help you create the new movie of your life.

When we really live in the present moment, the world begins to change. We see things that have been right in front of us that we've never noticed. We wake up from a world of separation and discover a world of interconnectedness. By paying attention, we lay fertile ground to plant our seeds of intention.

Director's Notes

🌟 You can create what you desire by being mindful of your surroundings, feelings, and thoughts. Set a phone reminder three times each day to bring your awareness back to the present moment.

🌟 If you have no awareness of what you are feeling and thinking, you may be thinking and feeling things that are of no service to you. Use the Five-Senses Check-In to stop the mental chatter about the past and the future, and ground yourself in the present moment.

❋ Being mindful helps you to be ready when Source delivers a message in the form of a serendipitous moment that will lead you toward your destiny.

❋ The 15-minute mindfulness exercises make you even more proficient at being here now.

Practice 2

MEDITATION: CULTIVATING CLARITY TO DISCOVER YOUR DREAMS

"Sun says, 'Be your own illumination.' Wren says, 'Sing your heart out, all day long.' . . . Stream says, 'Do not stop for any obstacle.' Oak says, 'When the wind blows, bend easily, and trust your roots to hold.' . . . Ant says, 'Small does not mean powerless.' Silence says nothing. In the quiet, everything comes clear. . . ."

— DANNA FAULDS

The first time I walked into a meditation retreat was at a Tampa, Florida, meditation center. I was surprised at the sparseness of the room. There were 12 black cushions sitting on 12 black mats, a few colored flags on the wall, and the teacher's meditation station at the front of the room. I was used to attending workshops at luxurious yoga studios with candles, wood flooring, gorgeous art on the walls, and water fountains in the corner.

This, in comparison, appeared downright dull. *Maybe it's intentionally designed that way so that there's no outside stimulation,* I thought.

We all took our seats, and the teacher took his. I admired the way he sat down, as if he were a humble king taking his seat on the throne. I was excited, too, and, for some reason, felt very grown up. I was about to sit in silence for three hours straight, and that seemed like a pretty grown-up thing to do.

That's right. I said three hours. It was going to be a challenge, but I love to challenge myself whenever I can.

I initially had rolled my eyes when Dr. Gurvit had suggested I attend the retreat. She told me that I'd be sitting for three hours at a time over the course of three days.

"I guess you don't have the courage to sit with yourself for that long," she challenged me.

"I am a spiritual warrior," I'd said. "And I can do anything I put my mind to."

I promptly pulled the retreat brochure out of her hand and called to register.

Now, sitting on the hard black cushion, I was questioning that act of bravery. The beginning of our first three-hour "sit" was officially announced by a gong. Out of nowhere, my thoughts started to pick up speed.

My back really hurts.

I wonder what they're serving for lunch.

How many minutes have passed?

I'm starving.

I should really rent The Devil Wears Prada.

I love Meryl Streep.

I wonder how many minutes have passed now.

I didn't know it was possible to think so many thoughts at once.

It was like the first day of a diet, when I suddenly crave pancakes, waffles, an omelet, and a chocolate malt. The day I tell myself that I'm not going to eat as much is the very same day that I want to pull up a chair and eat directly out of the refrigerator.

It's like that in meditation, too. The moment you know you're supposed to be slowing down your thoughts, they pick up with such speed that you can barely keep up.

But back to my mat:

There I was, as uncomfortable as possible, sitting on a hard cushion. About three minutes passed before I opened an eye and looked around the room for someone to save me. I glanced sideways at my fellow meditators. I couldn't believe how peaceful they all seemed. No one moved. They sat with perfect posture, looking like rows of good soldiers in semi-comatose states of bliss.

I wanted to kick them.

I closed the eye I had opened for spying and went back to my dizzying whirl of thoughts. I felt out of control. I was a powerless victim of my own wildly racing mind. This was shaping up to be the longest three hours of my life.

Just before he rang the gong, our teacher said, "Every time you have a thought, simply notice it. Do not label it good or bad, right or wrong. Just say the word *thinking,* and then gently come back to your breath."

So I sat up as straight as I could, and as my thoughts sped by, I chanted at each one, *Thinking, Thinking, Thinking.* I figured I'd just wind up chanting *Thinking* for three straight hours. The mere idea made me want to laugh out loud. Suddenly, a deep giggle began to rise up inside my belly. It was working up through my esophagus and threatening to come out of my mouth.

I opened one eye to stop my inner giggling before it became an audible laugh that would bother the other students. They were all still sitting motionless and peaceful.

I finally decided to step out of the class. I went outside and laughed so hard that I couldn't stand up straight. I nearly fell onto the grass in a fit of hysteria. Then I walked around the block several times, recovering from my bout of silliness.

I started thinking about the time when I was filming the HBO movie *Recount.* I was portraying a college professor, surrounded by college-age students who were hired as extras. Between takes, they were getting a little rowdy. Then, out of nowhere, the director yelled, "Quiet on the set!" The college kids froze and stared back as if they'd been caught stealing red-handed. The crew members froze, too. Even I froze.

A stillness settled over the set.

As this *aha* moment settled into my brain, I made my way back to the meditation center. I quietly crept back in and made my way to my seat. Every time my thoughts got out of control, I imagined myself sitting in the director's chair. So I imagined myself picking up my horn and powerfully saying to myself, *Quiet on the set!*

It worked. I slowed my thoughts and quieted them down.

I was proud of myself by the time the last gong sounded. I made it through a total of 18 hours of silence over three long days. I'd survived mental boot camp. By my last day, I had no more thoughts to think. I had exhausted them all.

I had also laid the foundation for my daily meditation practice. Sitting for ten minutes each day after making it through three-hour sessions was going to be a piece of cake!

What Is Meditation?

Meditation is the practice of focusing our concentration on breath, sound, or objects. It is designed to cultivate peace, clarity, and wisdom, and it originated from the human need to seek answers to the most universal of questions:

※ *Why are we here?*

※ *Where did we come from?*

※ *What is the purpose of our existence?*

While science explores questions of the universe by searching outward, meditation explores the spiritual side of the same quandaries by going inward. One of the oldest forms of meditation, called Tantric meditation, was developed more than 5,000 years ago to understand the conscious mind. Researchers speculate that primitive hunter-gatherer societies may have discovered meditation and its altered states of consciousness while staring into the flames of their fires.

Over thousands of years, meditation has evolved into a structured practice in many religions and cultures around the world, but there is a huge misperception about it among the general public. Many people believe that in order to be good at it, you must stop thinking altogether.

That's not true.

What meditation really does is slow down our thoughts. It provides a space between them where the mind can rest and Source can enter. It is in that space that we access our own wisdom and insight, as well as create access to Universal knowledge. In this sense, meditation is a way to explore the hidden parts of the mind and spirit.

The very act of stopping outer distractions offers the chance to delve inward and explore.

In nearly all its forms, meditation involves single-minded focus and concentration. Whether focusing on the rhythms of a walking meditation or those of music, the practice is about increasing our innate ability to concentrate. Some meditators practice guided meditation or a relaxing mantra, others simply focus on breath, but they're all striving for the same goal.

I once got a fortune cookie that said, "The most powerful thing in the Universe is a focused mind." I couldn't agree more.

Why Meditate?

Think about how we care for ourselves. We think it's not only acceptable, but also healthy, to join a gym and exercise our physical muscles every day. Too many of us, though, don't give the same attention to work out our minds.

Meditation is like taking your mind to the gym. You become the master of your thoughts and control where they go, as well as where they take you. In this way you can also hold yourself in the present moment, where peace lives.

I've witnessed hundreds of students transform as they used the practice of meditation for their own benefit. My student Jessica was able to wean herself off antianxiety medication after learning meditation. She had suffered from obsessive thoughts and constant worry, as her mind was constantly focused on thoughts that her boyfriend would betray her, her boss would fire her, or she would get into a car accident. Even when she was on medication, she had endured at least one panic attack a day.

Within two weeks of beginning meditation, Jessica decided not to sit for just ten minutes, but to meditate for a half hour each day. She instantly saw the benefits of becoming the master of her thoughts. She also quickly learned to train her mind to stay in the present moment. When her mind tried to carry her back to worry about the future, she used meditation. Each week, she arrived at class a little calmer, more focused, and less anxious. By our final class together, she was an entirely different person.

Meditation is not always a replacement for medication, but for Jessica it became a way to slowly end her dependence on pharmaceuticals and use her mind to set aside her worry. Whether you are battling anxiety, as she was, or struggling with some other energy that is holding you back, the simple steps outlined in the upcoming meditation instruction can make a real difference. By sitting in silence each day, you become the master of your mind. Dr. Herbert Benson of The Benson-Henry Institute for Mind Body Medicine, which is affiliated with Harvard University and several Boston hospitals, reports that meditation can reduce chronic pain, anxiety, high blood pressure, serum cholesterol level, and substance abuse; increase intelligence-related measures; reduce post-traumatic stress syndrome in Vietnam veterans; and lower blood cortisol levels initially brought on by stress. Meditation also brings us closer to ourselves and to the pulse of life.

But what does it have to do with directing your destiny?

Meditation goes hand in hand with manifestation. Every day, when we practice observing our thoughts, withholding judgment, and coming back to the breath, our minds become full of the awareness that we are part of a field of consciousness.

That field is Source.

When we reach this awareness, we also realize that we are all creators. Each moment between our thoughts provides access to our personal power and gives us clarity about what we want to manifest.

Remember the glass of sand and dirt that my therapist shook up? That's your mind, all day long. We all have endless dialogues with ourselves. We focus on regretting the past, worrying about the future, and planning things that will likely never happen. We allow judgmental thoughts to control our views of who we are and what we are doing. Meditation helps the dirt and sand to settle. Things become crystal clear. That clarity of mind is precisely what we all need to become the writer, producer, and director of our dreams.

When we don't know what we want in life, Source doesn't know what to give us. But when we are focused and clear about our desires, Source synchronizes with those thoughts and delivers exactly what we have asked for.

In order to manifest our dreams, we need to be quiet enough to hear what we really want.

How to Meditate

Even if you're meditating for just ten minutes each day, it is important to have an area in your home specifically designed to do just that. Find a room or corner of your home where you will not be disturbed. Get a comfortable cushion to sit on, a small table for flowers, and a candle. This will be your "meditation station."

Set up your station in a way that inspires you. Then, choose a time to do your meditation each day. This will form the foundation of your daily manifestation practice and should be a natural part of your routine for the next four weeks. Then, follow these steps:

1. Sit comfortably on a cushion or chair with your spine straight. (If you are on a cushion, sit with your legs loosely crossed. If you are in a chair, keep your legs uncrossed and your feet flat on the floor.)

2. Adjust yourself until you are in an upright position.

3. Put your hands facing down on your thighs, with your fingers relaxed.

4. Do the Five-Senses Check-In, and be sure you are in the present moment.

5. Close your eyes, tuck in your chin, and relax your jaw.

Next, place your mind on your breath and your *mantra*, which is a word or sound repeated to aid concentration during your meditation. I use the *Om* and *Ah* mantra. As I inhale, I silently say the primordial sound of the universe: *Om*. When I exhale, I do the same with the sound *Ah*. I chose *Ah*, because this sound is present in nearly every religious word for God:

- Ra
- Ta
- Krishna
- Rama
- Buddha
- Mahanta
- Brahma
- Atva
- Shiva
- Jehovah
- Allah
- God

When you meditate, choose a mantra that resonates with you. For many first-time meditators, it is easier to concentrate on words than to focus solely on the breath. Here are a few other mantras you might also consider using:

⁕ *In* on the in breath and, *Out* on the out breath

⁕ *Here* on the in breath, and *Now* on the out breath

⁕ *Smile* on the in breath, and *Relax* on the out breath

⁕ *Deep* on the in breath, and *Slow* on the out breath

If your mind begins to race, remember to call, *Quiet on the set!* Then return to your breath and mantra. Follow your breath as it goes in and out. Follow the sound of your chosen mantra in and then out.

I like to work with one mantra at a time. I usually use one for about a month and then switch to a new one.

With dedication to a meditation practice, you will become the director of your thoughts.

Overcoming Obstacles in Meditation

It is normal to encounter some obstacles in daily practice. Below are some useful antidotes that Dr. Gurvit gave me; I have modified them to help you resolve the most common obstacles you might encounter when you are trying to manifest through meditation.

Obstacle 1: Procrastination and Laziness. You walk by your meditation station and think, *I'll do that later.* Then, "later" never comes.

The Antidote: Build character and discipline. Give yourself a pep talk. Say to yourself, *I don't need to continue living this way. By invoking willpower and discipline, I can manifest my dreams.* Look in the mirror and tell yourself, *I refuse to keep making excuses.* Have an eye-to-eye conversation with yourself about the life you are intent on building, for this can make all the difference in the world.

Remember to not be discouraged. For most people, getting started is the hardest part. As you begin to see the benefits of your daily meditation, the unstoppable momentum that comes with it will energize you. Soon, meditating will be as habitual as brushing your teeth each day.

Obstacle 2: Boredom. For some people, meditation can seem like a grueling task. Perhaps you cannot wait for it to be over, glance around the room in search of a distraction, or continuously check your timer.

The Antidote: Allow yourself to be bored. In the beginning, it's necessary to surrender to the boredom. Stop the judgment. But ask yourself why you cannot seem to sit still for ten minutes. If you listen closely to your inner voice, you may be surprised by the answer.

If you stay with the practice, boredom will become awe. I promise.

Obstacle 3: Fear, Anxiety, or Anger. Meditation can sometimes bring long-buried emotions to the surface. They're distractions. It takes great courage to sit with yourself while intense feelings are coming to the surface. These are times for fearless warriors.

Remember: Fearlessness is not the absence of fear; it is the presence of bravery. This practice takes bravery and, above all, compassion for yourself.

The Antidote: Make friends with your fear. We cannot simply run from what scares or angers us. If we have the tools to move through those things, we reach the other side much faster.

Give yourself permission to feel uncomfortable. Ask yourself, *What's the worst that could happen? Where is this fear coming from?* Confront your emotions. When you do, it can lead to healing.

Obstacle 4: Fantasyland. Your ego may feel threatened when you begin to meditate. In fact, it will do anything to keep you from the enlightenment that meditation brings. It often does so by projecting a fantasy or tantalizing distraction onto your mind. If you fall prey to the ego's tricks, you may spend your entire time fantasizing, and not really meditate at all.

The Antidote: Just say no. Recognize that your ego is at work, and respond with a firm *Not right now.*

Obstacle 5: Sleepiness.

The Antidote: Think about something enticing for a few minutes. You will almost instantly perk up. Chances are that you aren't really tired at all, but your ego is once again trying to sabotage your meditation.

The Ultimate Antidote: Return to breath. Whenever a distraction arises, acknowledge it and return your attention to your breathing.

Try the meditation outlined in this book for four weeks. You may also consider joining a meditation group or attending a retreat, which is a good way to stay focused and find others who can offer support when you're frustrated or need motivation.

During Week I, you will need to set up a meditation station, do the Five-Senses Check-In, and practice sitting in silence for ten minutes each day. Remember to read Practice 3 before beginning your Soulwork for all three practices in Week I.

Director's Notes

- ❋ Meditation is necessary for you to become the director of your destiny. It gives you the clarity to write the screenplay of your life.

- ❋ Meditation will assist you in becoming the master of your thoughts. It will teach you tools to help you stop worrying about the future and regretting the past. You will create space in your brain for more clarity, creativity, and joy.

- ❋ Meditation gives you access to your own intuition and the universal wisdom of Source.

Practice 3

JOURNALING: CULTIVATING SELF-AWARENESS TO WRITE YOUR DREAMS

"Journaling your truth takes fierce courage,
but it will also make you braver."

DONNA JENSON (MY MOTHER)

Our work together may bring you into a world where you do not initially feel at home. Students always fall into one of two categories: those who identify themselves as artists and are already in touch with the creative energy that's needed to be a writer; and those who do not believe they are artistic or creative, or that they have the necessary skills to be a writer.

If you are in the second category, grab a pen and some paper. In all capital letters, write:

I AM NOT AN ARTIST.
I AM NOT CREATIVE.
I AM NOT A WRITER.

Done? Great. Now throw it in the trash.

Why? Because you *are* the artist of your life, the creator of your dreams, and the writer of your destiny. There is no room for argument. It can be no other way.

Journaling: Access to Within

Writing—in this case, journaling and recording your deepest thoughts by picking up a pen and pouring everything you think and feel onto the page—provides access to your truth, dreams, and inner wisdom. By asking questions about all that has been buried within you, your pen reveals something magnificent: the real you. Even if your writing will not win a Pulitzer or doesn't have the inspired touch of Rumi, it will bring out revelations that will surprise you.

Journaling is the act of putting pen to paper for the pure act of doing so. This act becomes less about being a good writer and more about the catharsis of getting thoughts out in a tangible way. Authors must write to earn a living. Job seekers must write cover letters to get an interview. Government staffers must write speeches to help establish the presence of an elected official. But journaling is different from all of these. While formal writing must be free of grammatical errors and spelling mistakes, what we're doing together has no rules. Journaling gives you permission to express yourself in any manner you choose. And unless you decide to share, it's for your eyes only.

And because it is only for you, journaling gives you permission to allow whatever crosses your mind to land on the page. It's therefore the kind of writing that comes from deep within. It does not matter if you make a spelling mistake or whether your composition seems awkward or profound.

In order to excavate what lies deep within, however, you need to dig to the bare bones of what lies inside. Only real questions will bring real answers. Remember, like attracts like. To access yourself, you must ask yourself the following:

* *Who am I, really?*
* *What do I want?*
* *What dreams do I want to create?*

32

You'll get the best answers when you are quiet and clear. And since journaling requires you to spend time alone in a safe place, it will allow you to find those qualities for yourself.

Though journaling doesn't always make sense or lead to anything significant or meaningful, writing through the nonsense will help you to find answers to these questions. Eventually, it will get you to the gold.

Why Journal?

Journaling is an excellent tool for intellectual, psychological, and spiritual growth. It moves you closer to your real feelings. Confusion becomes clarity when the thoughts and feelings within us are written down. Transferring our inner dialogue onto the page fosters a new perspective. Given enough time, journaling helps us find our true voice.

I have been journaling, off and on, since I was ten years old. Before it became a daily practice for me, it was a way to express myself. I turned to my journal when I fell in love, filling up pages with the name of my latest love interest, surrounding his name with drawings of hearts and poetry.

Whether it reveals elation or pain, journaling is cathartic. The words come in a rush and release with a flow. It helps us figure things out and provides a place to house our emotions.

Keeping a journal also connects us to our intuition and helps us make decisions. The Oracle at Delphi wisely counseled to "Know thyself." Journaling is a path to that knowing.

My client Madaline was unable to move forward in her new after-school yoga and meditation business for young people. She could not think of a name for the program. She had asked everyone she knew what they thought the name should be and wound up with 20 names that she didn't like at all.

I told Madaline to tap into her intuition, and the name would be there. I suggested she write, "The name of my program is . . ." at the top of her journal before bed. Then, when she woke up the next morning, she was to put pen to paper and start writing without thinking.

The very next morning, she wrote, "The Mindful Playground." Her work was done!

I use journaling in my own manifestation practice. It's another way to explore who I am and what I really want. It also takes courage.

When we take on mindfulness, meditation, and journaling practices, we become warriors. When we sit quietly and turn inward to journal, the truth we've been hiding comes to the surface. When that happens, we have three choices: push it back down, accept it, or shift it.

In addition to this book, there are almost unlimited resources about the practice and benefits of journaling. One of my favorites is *Opening Up: The Healing Power of Expressing Emotions,* by James Pennebaker. A psychologist and researcher, Pennebaker believes that regular journaling strengthens our immune cells, as well as helps combat the symptoms of asthma and arthritis. He has even found that writing about stressful events helps us come to terms with them, reducing their impact on our health.

People who journal every day have lower rates of depression, blood potassium, and even body weight.

In short, journaling is healthy.

The act of writing accesses the left side of the brain, which controls analytical and rational thought. While the left side of the brain is occupied, the right side is free to create, intuit, and feel.

Journaling can also clear mental blocks and allow access to your total brainpower. That, in turn, allows you to better understand yourself, others, and the world around you. It's also a powerful tool for manifesting what you want from Source. It paves the way to clarity and understanding so that you can articulate what you want.

Keeping a journal allows us to identify patterns of improvement and growth over time. When something seems insurmountable, we can write about it and later look back to rediscover the process through which we overcame our obstacles. The different practices I've outlined for you in this chapter will help you develop a daily practice.

Many people find it best to write before they've fully woken up in the morning. The inner critic is not yet alert, and the creative flow is often greater. Others enjoy an evening practice to reflect on the day.

Some of my students report practicing journaling before their manifestation and meditation sessions (which you will find introduced after the practices). It's entirely up to you. Whatever works best is the right choice. The only commitment required is five minutes each day. (But if you're inspired to keep going, write until your pen runs dry.)

When you journal, you can be as outrageous as your heart desires. You can express anger without hurt, dream your biggest "What if . . . ?" dreams, and uncover the tender parts of yourself for healing and growing. Your paper will not judge you, criticize you, or belittle you. It is only there to support you. All you have to do is come back to it and spend some more time enjoying that support.

The Five Journaling Exercises

Outlined here are five journaling exercises to choose from each day. You may find that you enjoy freewriting or journaling at a specific time. Morning may work best, or you may find evening practice more fulfilling. These five exercises allow you to experiment with each and choose the one that resonates best with you.

Remember to practice journaling for at least five minutes each day for the entire four weeks.

Freedom Writing

Set a timer for five minutes and put pen to paper. Write anything and everything. Do not edit what you've written or check for grammar or spelling mistakes. And no matter what, do not stop.

If your mind goes blank, rewrite the line you just wrote. Repeat this process until a new thought flows from your pen. As you continue, something magical will happen: you will get in touch with your truth. Then, there's no looking back.

I recommend trying Freedom Writing first. If you are new to journaling, you will have a lot to say. When you journal, you may often say things you don't really mean. Simply allow yourself to feel that way at that particular moment. Some students worry that someone may read their journals and see their private feelings. If you have this fear, take a few precautions.

One of my students, in the midst of a difficult separation, wrote on a yellow legal pad. She was afraid that her soon-to-be ex-husband would read it, so each day after finishing her journaling, she would rip out what she had written, tear it up, and throw it out.

You might also consider buying a small safe to lock up your journal. Some students keep their journals at work or in their cars. All that matters is that you express your feelings each day.

After you've tried Freedom Writing for a week or so, move on to one of the prompts in the following list. All you need to do is set your timer and begin—and don't stop until the timer chimes. If you feel motivated to journal longer than five minutes, keep going. If you feel stuck, use these prompts to help you get through times when you're not sure what to write.

Put any of these prompts at the top of your page and write for five minutes:

✳ I am obsessed with . . .

✳ I have noticed . . .

✳ I am aware of . . .

✳ I know this is true . . .

✳ What I need now is . . .

✳ If I could not fail, I would . . .

✳ If I only had a year to live, I would . . .

✳ I need to accept . . .

✳ I need to change . . .

✳ I feel light when . . .

✳ I feel dark when . . .

✳ I have lost . . .

✳ I have found . . .

✳ I remember . . .

✳ I can't remember . . .

Or:

✳ Choose a piece of music and write to its rhythm.

✳ Select a quote or line from a book that moves you, write it at the top of the page, and begin.

✳ Open a book, magazine, or dictionary and find a word that inspires you. Write it at the top of the page and begin.

✳ Look at a picture book or choose a photo that intrigues you, and write whatever comes to mind.

✳ Take an old photo out and write about the memory attached to it.

Or:

✳ Write a letter to yourself.

✳ Write a letter to someone who has betrayed you. (But don't send it!)

✳ Write a letter to your current self from your 90-year-old self.

✳ Write a letter from your seven-year-old self to your current self.

My student Julie shared this impromptu journal entry with me after completing three of my courses. She gave me permission to share it with you. It was written from the prompt "I am aware of . . ." and was completed in five minutes. (For authenticity, this journal entry has not been edited for grammar, spelling, or flow. Remember that your journal entries should also be free from the constraints of the usual "rules" of writing.)

> *I am aware of . . .*
>
> *The shift that has taken place inside me. As I look back at some of my journal entries from months past, I see how much I have transformed and grown into this enlightened, powerful, intuitive being. I see how much I have let go of things that caused me depression or unwanted stress, and I feel a peace inside me that I rarely have ever felt before. I feel a certainty and a*

confidence that I have never known, and it comes from my heart, from a place of truth.

I am aware that a new me has emerged, and I now see clearly how all of the work I have been doing with Jen has affected me, on a cellular level. I see how all of my daily practices of meditation and prompt journaling, like this, and setting intentions and affirmations—reading them aloud with fervor & zest.

. . . All of these practices have brought me clarity & honesty about who I am and what I am truly intended for.

And what's so amazing is that I am finally understanding what detachment means. I have been on a mission for over a year to really wrap my brain around this, and suddenly, I got it. I got that it's not about getting the "things" that I want or that I thought I wanted: my home in Positano, my antique Mercedes 450 SL convertible, my Oscar, my starring role in a film with Russell Crowe. . . . It's about "intending" to make an impact on people's lives by doing the things that I love and knowing what I am meant to do. It's about setting intentions that come from my heart and soul, not from my ego.

I am aware that in the past, all of my intentions and affirmations were from my ego, and now they are from a place of honesty and truth, and because of that, I am seeing miracles happen every day—things that I never imagined could happen to me. And the funniest thing is that most of the things that are happening are so much bigger and better than what I originally thought I wanted.

Porthole Writing

For centuries, scientists have used a brilliant technique that provides access to insights in a remarkable way. I have remixed their practice, and I call it Porthole Writing. There is an access point—a porthole—between when we are conscious and when we are unconscious, and we can use this time to our advantage.

Thomas Edison, Albert Einstein, and others used the time between wakefulness and deep sleep to tune in to the creative genius of the subconscious mind. Known as the *Twilight State,* this is the magical technique that Edison used while discovering electricity.

Supposedly, Edison would sit up in his chair, hold a fork in his hand, and place a metal plate on the floor. The moment he fell asleep, the fork would slip out of his hand and hit the plate, and the noise would wake him from the Twilight State. That was when he had his greatest epiphanies about electricity.

You can use the Twilight State in your writing practice to open a porthole to your creative mind.

Before you go to sleep at night, choose one of the porthole prompts, write it at the top of a journal page, and, the moment you wake up, respond to it for five minutes.

There is only one rule: You cannot stop writing. If you run out of things to write, start over and write the prompt again until a new response emerges.

Feel free to create your own porthole prompts, too, if there are specific ideas that you find inspiring or helpful.

Porthole Prompts. Begin with "Now that I know I am limitless and have the power to create anything I want . . ." and then use any of the following prompts:

- ✳ . . . the home that I will live in next looks like . . .
- ✳ . . . the career that would most fulfill me is . . .
- ✳ . . . the love relationship I will create will be like . . .
- ✳ . . . my body will feel and look like . . .
- ✳ . . . the next vacation I take will be . . .
- ✳ . . . the relationship I build with my family will look like . . .
- ✳ . . . the new adventures I will embark on with my friends will be . . .
- ✳ . . . the balanced and connected relationship I have with Source will look like . . .

Morning Porthole Writing

In addition to giving you access to the Twilight State, Morning Porthole Writing will allow you to remember your dreams, which are messages about your true feelings. As you learn to direct your future life, it's critical that you tap into these powerful and transformative signs.

Place your journal and pen by your bed. The moment you wake up, set your timer for five minutes and write in a stream-of-consciousness fashion. Do not stop. If you cannot think of anything to write, repeat the last line you wrote until a new thought comes.

The morning practice is especially illuminating, because your inner critics have not woken up. You will not try to censor what you say, and you will have complete freedom to write your truth.

Prompts are not necessary for the morning practice. Simply let your mind go, and your hand will take over. There will be a different revelation almost every time.

You might write about a dream you've just had. Or, you may start the day's to-do list. Sometimes, venting is necessary first thing in the morning. Other times, you may wake up with brilliant ideas that, if not immediately captured, may be fleeting.

I've used the morning practice to help formulate chapters for this book, jot down ideas for new retreats, and give birth to new tools for my students.

Each time you do the morning practice, you'll likely find at least one sentence or idea that is a true pearl of wisdom. As you do the practice more often, you'll string your own beautiful pearl necklace.

Remember, this is a practice. Not all of us will discover electricity on the first morning. But each of us will, over time, tap into the personal brilliance that helps us manifest our destiny.

Future-Self Writing

The Creative Insight Journey contains an exercise called "Meet Your Future Self." It has long been a favorite among my students. It was also a life-altering experience for me. The meditation takes you on a journey 20 years into the future. There, you see the home you live in and meet your future self.

According to the Retrocausation Theory of quantum physics, our past, present, and future are not happening in a linear fashion, as previously thought. In Newtonian science, things happen in a linear way, in chronological order. For example, we are born, then grow old, and eventually die. Events in our lives appear as the past, present, and future. This feels real and concrete, because we experience it every day. Retrocausation, however, shows us that time isn't linear at all. In fact, all is happening simultaneously.

Laboratory studies show that you can perceive future events before they occur. Dr. Daryl J. Bem, a social psychologist at Cornell University, conducted a series of studies that was published in the *Journal of Personality and Social Psychology*. Across nine experiments, Bem explored the idea that the brain has the ability to not only reflect on past experiences, but also anticipate future experiences. This ability for the brain to "see into the future" is often referred to as *psi phenomena*. Historical accounts are full of such actions, in the form of precognitive dreams, spontaneous healing, synchronicities, and past-life memories. If we can "see into the future," the future already exists—which means there is, right now, an older, wiser you living in the future. By cultivating a relationship with this future self, you can access wisdom that you typically would not have for decades to come.

When I first visited my future self, she gave me a gift and a name. I have never forgotten either.

The gift was a golden pen. When I asked what it was for, she told me to look around. I saw a bookshelf with many volumes. I looked back at her, confused.

"You, my dear, are going to write those books," she said.

I had never written a book before. Now, you are holding my first one. Before I left, I asked my future self for her name.

"Grace," she replied.

Shortly thereafter, I changed my professional last name from Safina (my ex-husband's name) to Grace. By doing so, I was able to step into the power of her field.

I now have a journal titled "Channeling Grace." Each time I visit with my future self in meditation, I journal everything she tells me. I ask questions, and she answers in words, symbols, or photographs. Inevitably, I find that what she has said comes to fruition.

Your relationship with your future self is a powerful one that will allow you to access answers and insights that you've been searching for. When many of us have a major decision to make, we take a grand poll by asking our mothers, partners, siblings, and friends, "What do you think I should do?" We usually get a different answer from each person and end up frozen and confused.

Instead remember *YAK: You Always Know.*

You always have the wisdom you need inside of you. If you feel the need to ask for someone's advice, ask yourself first. By asking your future self, you have instant access to a wise person right inside you.

"Meet Your Future Self" Meditation

It is important to answer the questions at the end of this exercise immediately after completing the meditation. Find a quiet place where you will not be interrupted. If you are inspired by the results, consider buying your own special journal or "Channeling" diary.

To practice this exercise, listen to the future-self meditation. You can have someone read it to you aloud, record it yourself, or download a free MP3 from my website at **www.thecenterofgrace.com /meditation**. Find a quiet place to lie down, and close your eyes as you listen to the guided meditation. Then, after it's over, choose one or more of the questions that follow the meditation to ask your future self. They are designed to guide you in an interview with your future self. Write each question on the top of the page. Also, think of a question that you would personally like to ask your future self. Then allow for an answer.

> *Imagine that you are walking along a beautiful riverbank. It is a perfect day. The birds are singing. You can feel the warmth of the sun on your face, and you feel safe and that all is well. As you walk along, you suddenly see a boat driven by a friendly captain. The captain pulls the boat along the shore and helps you in. You begin to sail down the river, but you notice that this is a different kind of river. This is the river of time.*
>
> *Five years pass. Ten years pass. Fifteen years pass. Twenty years pass.*

The friendly captain pulls the boat along the riverbank and helps you out. He points to the place where you live 20 years from now.

Where are you? Is it a city street, a country road, the mountains, the beach, or another country? This is yours. Paint it in.

You see the house. You knock on the door, and your future self answers. Look into that person's eyes. Those are your eyes. Look at that person's smile. Notice what your future self is wearing, including the jewelry, the clothes, and even the shoes.

Your future self brings you into one of the rooms in the home. You have created all of this. Look at the colors, textures, furniture, and fabrics.

Your future self asks you to sit down, and then leaves the room.

Eventually, your future self returns, carrying a beautifully wrapped gift. What has this person given you today? Ask your future self if there is any significance to this gift. Allow him or her to whisper the answer in your ear.

Now your future self looks you deeply in the eyes and asks, "What do you want to know?"

Ask your future self any question in your heart, or ask for wisdom or insight about your next steps on this journey. Allow the person to answer by talking or showing you symbols or photographs, or even by a running film.

Before you leave, ask your future self if there is one more thing he or she needs to tell you, or if there is something important that you need to know.

It's time to go.

Your future self walks you to the door. Before you leave, ask, "Is there a name I can call you when I come to visit, a name other than my own?"

Let your future self whisper this name in your ear. Give this person a hug and say that you will return.

Your future self thanks you and says to come back anytime you need questions answered or guidance. This person is your ally and is here to help.

Now, make your way back to the river, where the friendly captain is waiting. Board the boat and begin to sail.

Five years . . . 10 years . . . 15 years . . . 20 years . . . back to now.

Open your eyes.

Here are some good questions to use when you interview your future self:

Future-Self Interview Prompts

❋ *Who am I?*

❋ *What is my life's purpose?*

❋ *What are my greatest gifts and talents?*

Relationship Prompts

❋ *What do you think about the person I am in a relationship with?*

❋ *Is this relationship healthy for me?*

❋ *What should I do about this relationship?*

Prompts for Starting a Relationship

❋ *What is blocking love from coming into my life?*

❋ *What qualities should I look for in a partner?*

❋ *What habitual patterns should I work on before beginning a new love relationship?*

Guidance Questions

❋ *What would be good next steps for my career?*

❋ *What steps should I take to improve my health?*

❋ *What would be good next steps for _____ (fill in blank)?*

Evening Reflection Writing

I also love to journal in the evening. The texture of night can help facilitate a state of reflection. As you consider those aspects that make up who you are and what you want to be, elaborate on the topics. Reflect on how the answers you've received should influence the new life you'll write for yourself. Each answer includes a clue about who you are and what you desire. It's your own personal detective story. Dig in, look around, and experience the story data that's necessary for your screenplay.

Do not set a timer when using these prompts. Instead, pause and reflect. Take your time.

Journal Prompts for Self-Realization (No Timer)

Make these lists a part of your evening journaling:

- ※ Ten things you love to do.
- ※ Five activities worth staying up all night for.
- ※ Five things you loved as a child.
- ※ Five favorite television programs or five favorite books.
- ※ Ten of your favorite people, real or fictional. Taking this a step farther, you could then list five personality traits that you find appealing about each of the ten people. (Note whether there are characteristics that all or most of your favorite people have. Are they qualities that you'd like to have?)
- ※ Ten places you love or would love to visit.
- ※ Five things you want to create.
- ※ Ten material objects that you love or would love to have.
- ※ Ten ideas or concepts that fill your mind, spark your imagination, or excite your curiosity.
- ※ Five things you hope to accomplish in your lifetime.

These lists give extraordinary clues about what inspires you, motivates you, and makes you feel alive. Look back at your lists often. Commit to doing more of these things.

You will be amazed at the insights you gain during journaling. You will discover more about who you are, and what does and does not serve you. You will also formulate powerful intentions that ultimately lead to collaboration with Source. In return, you can receive the unlimited gifts and abundance it offers you.

Remember to journal for at least five minutes each day during your four weeks of work with this program. If you continue to journal longer, the benefits will only increase in measure.

With your journal, you will always have a place to sort through thoughts and emotions. In return, you will open yourself up and allow creativity in. You will create space for your own wisdom and surprise, inspire, and delight yourself.

Director's Notes

※ Journaling is an excellent tool for intellectual, psychological, and spiritual growth. It helps move you closer to your real feelings. Confusion becomes clarity when we write down the thoughts and feelings swirling around in our hearts and minds.

※ Journaling is a tool for manifesting what you want from Source. It paves the way to clarity and understanding so that you can articulate what you want.

※ Cultivating a relationship with your future self provides you access to wisdom. Your future self is the older, wiser version of you who will never steer you wrong.

※ Keeping a journal allows you to track patterns and improve and grow over time. When current circumstances appear insurmountable, record them and look back on the process that led to a resolution.

Soulwork: Week I

Do the following for seven days:

※ Create a meditation station.

※ Buy a new journal.

※ Set a phone reminder to "be here now" three times each day. Notice where your mind is when the alarm goes off. Then bring yourself back to the present moment by doing the Five-Senses Check-In or taking three slow, deep breaths.

※ Do one 15-minute mindfulness exercise.

※ Choose one writing practice each day, and journal for five minutes. Use the "Meet Your Future Self" Meditation.

Week I: Daily Meditation Practice

What follows is the guided Week I daily meditation practice in written form. You should be sitting up, with your spine straight, for this meditation. You can have someone read it to you, you can record it yourself, or you can download a free MP3 version at **www.the centerofgrace.com/meditation**.

> *Start with the Five-Senses Check-In to drop into present-moment awareness and create a state of balance, clarity, and focus.*
>
> *First, evoke the sense of sight. Look around the room you are in. Notice the colors and textures. Move your eyes from object to object. Whenever you encounter a thought about the past or future, simply move your gaze to the next object in the room. Notice anything in the room that you've never seen before.*
>
> *What do you see? Be in the room.*
>
> *Now, close your eyes and evoke the sense of smell. Breathe in deeply. Notice if you smell anything specific in the room. Perhaps it is something you cooked earlier, the scent of a candle, or the breeze coming in through the open window.*

Next, evoke the sense of sound. Notice what sounds are coming from the room you are in. Now, notice any sounds coming from outside the room. Try listening through just your right ear and then your left.

Now, evoke the sense of touch. Notice how your feet feel on the floor. Notice how your clothing feels on your body and how the air feels on your cheek.

Finally, evoke the sense of taste. Gently glide your tongue along the top of your teeth, and swallow.

Now just be.

Now begin your ten-minute meditation session.

To begin, take three long, deep breaths. Straighten your spine and rest your hands lightly on your thighs. Begin to follow your breath in and out.

When a thought comes in, simply notice it. Do not label it as <u>good</u> or <u>bad</u>. Simply say <u>Thinking</u> to yourself, and gently return to your breath.

You may use a mantra as you meditate. On the in breath, silently say <u>in</u>, and on the out breath, say <u>out</u>. Or say <u>here</u> on the inhalation and <u>now</u> on the exhalation.

Now begin.

Sit quietly for ten minutes of silence.

You have now completed your daily meditation routine.

BECOMING THE PRODUCER OF YOUR DREAMS

Tools Needed for Week II:

✳ *A stack of brightly colored three-by-five-inch cards*

✳ *A blank piece of paper and colored markers*

The job of a film producer is to navigate the creation of the film from start to finish. The producer helps turn a story into a screenplay, and is charged with hiring key crew members, including the director. A producer oversees budgets, hires editors, and helps market the film to the public. Without the producer, a film can easily fall apart. It is the producer's job to look at the big picture and manage nearly every aspect of production.

During the days when I owned an independent film company, I wore many hats, from screenwriter to actress to wardrobe consultant. I was also the producer on every film the company made. In this role, I had to make sure we hired the right people, shot in the right locations, and bought the right clothes for each actor to wear in each scene. In short, I had to make sure everything ran smoothly, from catering to scheduling. It involved keeping every ball in the air and every player in alignment.

I quickly learned that happy people make a happy set. And happy sets, in turn, bring about great films.

Aligning Your Thoughts, Beliefs, and Feelings

In short, a producer's job is to keep a film's various components connected. You must do the same in order to become the producer of your own life.

How do you know when your life is well produced? It's when you love your work, find harmony in your relationships, and take time out for adventure. A life that's produced well is a life where things flow effortlessly and synchronize automatically with your goals. When you are in alignment with your true self, you will experience a natural flow that carries you from one breakthrough to another.

Inevitably, there are bumps in the road for even the most impeccably planned journeys. However, when your life is in alignment, you will gracefully move past them as you grow and transform.

What do you need to align in order to produce the movie of your dreams? What the Universal Law of Attraction is basically saying is that what we focus our thoughts, beliefs, and emotional frequency on is what we manifest into creation. Everything we think, believe, and feel must be congruent with each other. Your thoughts, beliefs, and emotions create a certain frequency, which in turn creates the movie of your life.

The Law of Attraction works by bringing to you the things you focus on. Those thoughts must be supported by a belief system in which everything is possible. You must know—deep within you—that you deserve a full and meaningful life. You must have absolute certainty that you deserve happiness. You must see it, believe it, and—most important—*feel* it in order to manifest it.

You must also use the language of your emotions to communicate directly with Source. When you do, the Law of Attraction is activated.

When I first saw the film *The Secret,* I was focused solely on my thoughts. I made a vision board and put my dreams on it. All I had to do, I thought, was settle into my couch, stare at my board, and think happy thoughts.

Unfortunately, under all those happy thoughts and positive thinking was a current of negative belief. I didn't believe I was powerful enough to manifest the life of my dreams. I didn't believe I would ever find my purpose. I also didn't believe I would ever find my spiritual partner.

My negative, limiting belief system was drowning out my positive intentions. I was thinking positively, but I didn't believe positively. As a result, I didn't feel positive emotions, and my dreams were not manifesting.

I was ignoring the other two core components of believing and feeling. My sole focus was on what I was thinking. In order to become the producer of our lives, we must acquire the tools to focus on all three. Their alignment is key to manifesting our dreams.

There are two other tools that play a critical role in aligning what you are thinking, believing, and feeling. The first is about understanding how to observe yourself by stepping back and seeing the big picture of your life. The second is about learning to cultivate personal power and fearlessness in order to tap into the courage you need to pursue what you desire.

Seeing the Big Picture: The Art of Self-Observation

By using the tools you learned to become the writer of your life, you can now expand and learn how to step even farther outside yourself to objectively observe your big picture.

Your big picture combines the thoughts you are thinking, the beliefs you are holding, and the emotions you are feeling. You must first be fully aware of your day-to-day thoughts, beliefs, and emotions to work with the Law of Attraction.

In order to see the big picture, you must first put aside judgments about yourself. Rather than beat yourself up for decisions you've made and actions you've taken (or not taken), you must recognize that you're someone who's now seeking a better life.

Self-observation is not about criticizing ourselves for things in the past that we can never change, but reflecting on what we can do to continue the process of transformation. When we're introspective, we often see things clearly for the very first time. We learn how we have judged ourselves. By letting go of that judgment, we realize what is and is not working. We quickly shift our perspectives and come into alignment with our best possible selves.

To do this, you must observe, assess, and conclude. When you do, you can make the necessary adjustments to choose new thoughts, beliefs, and feelings that activate the Law of Attraction. That, in turn, will deliver a new movie that you will *want* to star in.

I recently had a student who was a very up-close and loud talker. She was constantly invading the personal space of others, but she couldn't figure out why she didn't have many friends.

Diving in and working on the practices I'd given her, this individual began to see herself from an outsider's perspective. Through journaling, she realized that her childhood left her struggling to be heard, since she's one of eight children. That experience was the source of her abrasive form of communication. She began to understand that when she was compelled to interject a thought during a conversation, she felt she had to cut the other person off or risk never being able to speak at all.

She also recognized that, deep within, she believed that what she had to say wasn't important. She was repeatedly told as much as a child. Her feelings of anger and frustration were the result of feeling unheard growing up.

Upon realizing these things, my student asked for my opinion. She was correct, I affirmed, in her assessment of herself. I also told her that I, too, once came across as a very loud, sometimes-obnoxious New Yorker, but as I cultivated a softer approach to communicating, I found people to be much more receptive.

I also taught her a trick that I've used myself in addition to learning how to reprogram my personal belief system. I asked her to imagine a remote control that would allow her to cut the volume in half every time she started a conversation with another person.

"Back up a few feet so the remote can work, and turn your volume down," I said.

It did the trick. She began connecting with other students in the class. She learned to listen intently and then speak mindfully at a respectful distance that gave other students plenty of space. She formed friendships in class, and soon other students were inviting her out to dinner. It was a beautiful transformation to behold.

You'll find that you often have something others see that remains invisible to you. By honestly looking at the impact you have on others, you can make the change necessary to manifest a new life for yourself. New thoughts and new beliefs will put you in a new emotional frequency. Source will then bring everything you desire to fruition.

Cultivating Personal Power and Fearlessness

Being the producer of your life means that you will be called upon to step into your power.

Throughout our four weeks together, I will help you cultivate that personal power and fearlessness.

Many people are afraid of failure *and* success. That fear is the only thing between you and your dreams. Before you manifest your new life, you have to get that emotion out of the way. The tools in Week II will help you cultivate the power to do just that.

We are all afraid, but we also all have a choice: Allow our fears to paralyze us and obstruct us on the path to the life of our dreams, or look fear in the face and say, "I see you. I feel you. But I will not let you win."

Fear affects our thoughts, beliefs, and feelings. When we're scared about what might happen, or anxious about a worst-case scenario, Source picks up that frequency. The Law of Attraction then sends more fear and anxiety. We activate a perpetual process that can turn our lives into a horror film. To avoid this, we must identify what we are afraid of and then slowly overcome our fears. We can change our emotional frequency from fear to confidence.

For most of my life, I've had a fear of physically intimidating adventures. For example, I wouldn't swim in the ocean for more than a few minutes, because the theme music from *Jaws* would pop into my head, and I'd begin frantically swimming for the shore. I was also afraid of heights, roller coasters, elevators, and any activity that might result in breaking a nail.

That, I presume, is why I was blessed with a son.

Being mother to my son, Cole, has been my first real experience with a young male relative. I don't have any brothers, and was unsure how to deal with Cole as he grew older and more daring. As a child, I was an avid and quiet reader. I also played with Barbie dolls, dressed up, and put on shows. I was a girl, through and through.

In contrast, my son loves to do all of the "boardings"—skateboarding, snowboarding, and wakeboarding—as well as other adventurous activities.

I began my act of overcoming physical fear when Cole, his good friend Nick, and I went to a water park together. They insisted that I go on a ride with them. This particular ride puts everyone in pitch darkness, while moving side-to-side at what feels like a million miles an hour, and then drops you straight down a 40-foot slide.

"No, thank you," I said to them, smiling. "I'll read my book. Come get me when you are done, and we'll all go to the lazy river."

"Mom," my son said in a way I will never forget. "I don't think it's right that you always talk about fearlessness with your students when you are afraid of almost everything."

My jaw dropped. My son, who often comes to my workshops, had learned my lessons better than I had.

I pride myself on being fearless in life and going after my dreams and passions. I work as an entrepreneur, travel the world, and speak to audiences of hundreds of people. But my son was right: when it comes to the physical side of life, I am a total chicken.

"Okay, Cole," I said as my heart began to pound. "You're right. I would be a fraud if I didn't go on the ride. I'll do it."

He looked at me with complete surprise, as he'd never convinced me to do something so physically intimidating before.

"Really, Mom?" he asked with wide eyes. "You're really going to ride with us?"

"Yep," I said. "But let's go now, before I change my mind!"

"No, that's not the proper way to overcome your fear," he said. "You have to work your way up to it."

Clearly, my son could be *teaching* my classes at this point.

He asked, "Remember when I overcame my fear of the dark? I didn't just turn off all the lights one night and fall asleep. I worked my way up to it. The first few nights you shut off the overhead light, and I slept with the lamp on. The next night, I slept with just the night-light on. Then we just had the hall light on. *Then,* after about two weeks, I slept in the dark."

I had forgotten all about that.

He continued, "So we need to do the same thing for you. First you can ride the silly slide, then the small wave, and finally the ride you're really afraid of trying. How does that sound, Mom?"

It sounded pretty smart to me.

The first two rides were a piece of cake. When we got to the last one, though, I was terrified. During the 15-minute wait in line, I observed myself and watched my inner dialogue start to work in a really negative way. I suddenly noticed a very negative voice inside of me saying, *You're 40 years old. You have no business being on this ride. You'll break your neck.*

But my self-observer intervened, saying, *Think new thoughts. Say something different to Jen.*

So I started saying, *Oh wow, I wish this line would hurry up! I want it to be my turn! I can't wait to go on this ride. I love the rush I get from doing daring things.*

I was employing an important acting tool that I'd developed during my days on film sets: inner monologue. This tool allows you to think the internal thoughts that your character might have. In doing so, you become more connected to what your character is feeling and thinking, even when he or she isn't actually speaking.

It was working! My heart was not pounding, my hands were not sweating, and I was smiling.

When it was our turn in line, Cole asked with some concern, "Mom, are you sure you really want to do this? I don't want to force you if you're too scared."

I looked back at him and boldly said, "No way! Let's do this, baby!"

Surprisingly, I didn't even scream as I was wildly whipped around in pitch darkness.

Since that day, I've mustered up the courage to walk on hot coals, get certified to scuba dive, zip-line thousands of feet up in the air, and go on a level-4 white-water rafting excursion. If you had asked me to do any of these things a few years ago, I would have refused.

Overcoming my fear of physical adventures has given me more personal and professional courage, too.

So, what is it that takes you out of your personal power? What are the things that stop you from moving forward fearlessly? Think about them this week, and challenge yourself to do something that you normally wouldn't. It could be a physical challenge, like what I experienced, or a personal one, such as having a conversation that you've been avoiding or asking your boss for a raise.

As you're about to engage in whatever it is that scares you, change the inner monologue that goes on inside your head. Be excited about what you're about to do, instead of letting that negative voice keep you frozen in your fear. I promise that you will be surprised and delighted at how easy it is once you take the plunge.

Expanding the Practices

During Week II you will introduce two important add-ons to your daily practices of mindfulness, meditation, and journaling. First, you will focus on setting powerful intentions for cultivating positive thinking, which will help you speak your dreams. To that, you will also add the practice of reprogramming your belief system in order to cultivate the personal power to believe that your dreams are possible.

In Week III, you will focus solely on the third practice necessary to become the producer of your dreams. This is the practice of authentically acting to cultivate truthful emotions in order to feel your dreams. There is a separate week for this practice, because it is the most vital part of the entire process and deserves individual attention.

One of the most powerful things in the universe is a focused mind. So imagine the power of engaging the Law of Attention with the Law of Attraction for 15 minutes each day. Then imagine the power of focusing all your attention on your intentions. By using the power of your mind to raise your thoughts, beliefs, and feelings to a higher state, you can reach your greatest potential.

Your daily meditation and manifestation practice will become stronger as we add Week II and III practices to these already powerful tools. Your inner producer will learn to align your dreams and goals with a sure belief in your ability to manifest them.

The next two weeks are all about stepping into your power and producing the amazing new movie of your life. The practices are simple yet profound. Approach this work with the willingness to observe yourself and your life without judgment. Be open to dreaming big. Give yourself permission to let go of the limiting beliefs that no longer serve you.

Becoming the producer of your life will allow you to oversee your own big picture with a fresh perspective. You'll have a newfound awareness that will give you the tools to bring everything into alignment with courage, compassion, and confidence.

SETTING INTENTIONS: CULTIVATING POSITIVE THINKING TO SPEAK YOUR DREAMS

"Intention is a field of energy that flows invisibly beyond the reach of our normal, everyday habitual patterns. It's there, even before our actual conception. We have the means to attract this energy to us and experience life in an exciting new way."

— Dr. Wayne W. Dyer

On January 11, 2011, I set the following six intentions for the upcoming year:

✳ *I feel ecstatic that I am now a published Hay House author!*

✳ *I feel overjoyed that I am now selling out lectures and have waiting lists for my Creative Insight Journey classes!*

✳ *I feel excited that I am now fitting into my skinny jeans!*

✳ *I feel gratitude that I am now doing what I love and making a difference in the lives of others!*

※ *I feel happy that I am now living in the Rio Vista neighborhood, where there are lots of kids my son's age for him to play with!*

※ *I feel in awe that I am now part of a beautiful circle of friends who love and support me unconditionally!*

Exactly 11 months later, on November 11, 2011, I was running an OmLuxe retreat in Bali, when I suddenly realized that nearly all of my intentions had come true. And even though I was not yet a published Hay House author, this book is, of course, evidence that it would soon happen.

On that very auspicious evening of 11/11/11, my friend and business partner Pamela Jones and I—along with the guests on our retreat—were gathered around a small fire in a little village just outside the town of Ubud in Bali.

Roosters were crowing loudly. Dogs were barking wildly. The Balinese priest who had opened his home to us wiped yellow war paint on our foreheads and drew a red dot onto our third-eye points. The ten of us watched in awe as he prepared for a manifestation ceremony.

The priest explained that the fire would accelerate our manifestations. A large stone in front of the fire represented the gods, to which he gave an offering of coconut milk, sugar, rice, and honey. As he poured each ingredient over the stone, he chanted in his native tongue.

Then, it was our turn.

We were each given a bowl of rice and told to throw small handfuls of rice into the fire 700 times.

"Did you say 70 times?" I asked, hoping that I hadn't heard him correctly.

"No," he said. "700 times."

I looked apologetically at my students, who all seemed slightly concerned. Nonetheless, we had all signed up for this once-in-a-lifetime experience, and none of us was about to back out now.

The priest looked very seriously at all of us and said, "The first 300 times you throw the rice, silently say in your mind what you are now willing to surrender. Then, for the remaining 400 throws, ask for what you want."

I began to panic. What did I want? If I was going to ask for something 400 times, it would help to, you know, actually have it in mind. I realized that as the leader of the retreat, I had been too busy coaching my students to develop their own intentions and had not created new intentions for myself.

I did a quick scan of my life. My health was great—I had lost 20 pounds and was wearing my skinny jeans again. My son and I were living in Rio Vista, where he had quickly made friends with four boys his own age. I had submitted a book proposal to Hay House and was awaiting their answer. And my Creative Insight Journey classes were filling up all year. I even had a waiting list. All of that happened, in part, because of an amazing circle of friends.

What more could I want? I felt as if I were already starring in the best movie I'd ever seen. I was literally walking in my dreams.

Then it hit me. There was something still missing in my life: love.

Earlier that year, I had ended a relationship. At the same time, I also realized that I'd never been alone since I was 16. I had gone from relationship to marriage to relationship again, and never had taken a break. I knew it was past time for one.

I declared that for my 40th year, I would be on a "hy-datus," a term that my good friend Joanna Popper coined to mean a break from dating.

So, for all of 2011, I had been on my own. It was by choice, and it had been extremely uncomfortable at first. I hated walking into events without someone by my side. I was conditioned to believe I wasn't "somebody" unless somebody else loved me.

I would go to sleep, and also wake up, feeling lonely and anxious. It took every tool I had just to get through the first three months of my hy-datus. Then, I began to love being single! I had no one to think about except my son, and I was cultivating stronger friendships. I had more time to spend with my girlfriends, and I didn't have to shave my legs every day!

I began enjoying my time alone so much that I didn't even think about falling in love again. But on that night, around the Balinese fire, something deep inside told me it was time.

So, I began to throw my rice—700 times.

As sweat poured down my face from the blazing heat of the fire, I affirmed until I couldn't anymore.

With each pitch of the rice, I thought about the qualities I was looking for in my next spiritual partner. The words that came to mind when I was throwing rice that evening included *charismatic, confident, kind, ambitious, powerful, funny, adventurous, creative, handsome,* and *open-minded.*

I was careful not to become too attached to details like physical appearance, career, or material wealth. I just asked for the essence of who he was.

Exactly one month and two days later—on December 13, 2011—I met him. He had every quality I had asked for and then some. As I write now, it's eight months later, and we are living "happily ever now." I will be returning to Bali soon, this time with him by my side, for another life-changing retreat.

What Is an Intention?

An intention is simply an aim or purpose to do, be, or have something. It is essentially a goal or a dream. My mentor Julia Romaine shared a wonderful tool for understanding the difference in feeling between when we have or don't have an intention.

First, read this exercise and then put down the book for a moment. Casually walk to the other side of the room. Once you have finished your walk to the other side, come back to the book. Go ahead and do this now.

Now, do it again. This time, however, think about something you really want. Imagine that it's on the other side of the room. All you have to do is go over and get it. Before you walk across the room, envision the object in your mind. Go ahead.

Didn't that feel different?

The first time, you probably walked aimlessly across the room. You had no specific purpose or intention in mind. The second time, however, you likely felt energized, focused, and motivated. That is the power of intention.

Intentions are simply powerful thoughts that you intend to make reality. To begin working with them, you'll need to learn the practice

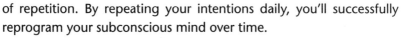

of repetition. By repeating your intentions daily, you'll successfully reprogram your subconscious mind over time.

Each time you're focused on your intentions, you're reinforcing your goal and creating a new blueprint in your mind.

In the story about how I joined my students in throwing rice into a Balinese fire pit, I was reinforcing my goal of finding a satisfying love relationship. In this case, I was performing a ceremony. Ceremonies, be they prayers conducted in a religious congregation or the types of rituals I share in this book, are all about setting intentions. By placing yourself in a certain place and partaking in a specific action in a specific way, you're creating that new blueprint. Of course, you don't necessarily need to throw rice into a Balinese fire pit 700 times to attain a satisfying love relationship or anything else, for there are plenty of ways to manifest your dreams.

In this program, you will set your intentions by incorporating a verbal repetition of them into your daily practice. This will create a tremendous amount of force behind them, and Source will respond to this power. Where you focus is where it will deliver.

Your Six Intentions

I usually work with six intentions at once. In numerology, this number is the most loving and harmonious of all numbers. I also use six because if we have too many intentions, we lose focus. At the same time, if we have too few, we tend not to stretch or challenge ourselves.

Each day, I take my six intentions, written out on three-by-five-inch cards, and read them aloud before beginning my meditation. This reminds me of what I'm up to. If you've ever made a New Year's resolution in January, only to notice by February that you haven't even started accomplishing it, then this method will be necessary and helpful. By reading your intentions every day, you remind yourself of what you've committed to.

You may even want to make more than one set. I have six intention cards by my bed, and I also keep others at my meditation station and in my car. When I'm stuck in traffic, I pull my cards out and read them. Doing so raises my emotional frequency and lowers my frustration.

It doesn't matter where or when you read your cards. The more you do, the faster they'll work for you.

For example, when I was using the daily intention *I feel thrilled that I am now a Hay House published author,* I hadn't yet accomplished that, but I repeated the intention frequently enough so that now I am.

Rate Your Life

By now, your meditation and journaling practices have started to bring the new movie of your life into focus. Your intentions are the script that you will use in that movie.

If you're still not clear about what you want to manifest, I suggest doing a life scan. Look at each area of your life and rate it on a 1-to-10 scale. If an area of your life is perfect, rate it at 10; if it's a complete debacle, score it at 1. A rating of 5 would be somewhere between the two extremes.

If any area is at 7 or below, create an intention for that area to help shift your experience.

Go ahead and rate the following categories of your life:

Health:	Home:
Love:	Friendships:
Finances:	Family:
Career:	Adventure/Fun/Travel:

If you have more than six areas ranked at 7 or below, choose the six that you want to work on first. If you have fewer than six areas in this range, make a second intention for one or more areas in your life that are not where you want them to be.

Formulating Intentions

Everything that happens is, of course, divinely timed. You cannot tell Source *when* something should happen, but you can certainly ask for *what* you want. In formulating your intentions, start with a goal you'd like to realize within the year. In the end, it may happen sooner or take a little longer, but start with something that's important and realistic.

Your intentions should be just outside your comfort zone. For example, the intention *I am a New York Times best-selling author* (a current intention of mine) would have been unrealistic before I wrote a book. However, it was more realistic, and also a bit outside of my comfort zone, to intend to be a published author, since I knew I could realistically achieve that goal first.

As you develop your intentions, keep in mind that you're on a journey. Ask Source for things that are possible, and don't set yourself up for disappointment or failure.

The categories that you just rated may help you decide which area of your life you would like to improve. For example and inspiration, I share six intentions from my student Julie, who's an actress. Every area of her life was rated at 8 and above except for three areas: career, finances, and friendship. She created two intentions for each of these three categories.

Career

— *I feel euphoric that I am now booking lead and supporting roles that are alongside actors, directors, and producers who excite me, stimulate me, and allow me to grow and challenge myself continuously.*

— *I feel elated that I now speak with Robert Newman, and other people with whom I have cultivated relationships, about doing roles in projects that I have been dreaming about.*

Finances

— *I feel ecstatic that I am now doing part-time work that provides me with the financial means to pursue my lifelong passion of acting, stress free.*

— *I feel at peace that I am now booking at least three national commercials each year that are bringing an abundance of money into my bank account.*

Friendship

— *I feel so happy that I am now part of an amazing group of friends.*

— I feel thrilled that I am now enjoying being someone's best friend. We laugh, we listen, and we have the best time together!

The Formula

You can follow a very simple formula when crafting an intention:

I *feel* [insert emotional state that you will feel when this intention comes to fruition] *that I am now* [insert goal].

Always use *I am* or *I have,* never *I want* or *I need.* Source is very literal. If you say *I want,* you will get more wanting. If you say *I need,* you will get more needing. However, if you say *I am,* as if it has already occurred, Source will deliver it to you.

It is possible, though, that you are not yet fully clear about what you want to create. If that's the case, manifest clarity by saying, *I feel overjoyed that I am now crystal clear about my life's purpose.* Here are some more examples of intentions from some of my other students:

* *I feel thrilled that I am now working my own hours and helping people by doing what I love.*

* *I feel grateful that I am now financially free.*

* *I feel proud that I now have a loving relationship with my daughter.*

* *I feel empowered that I am now a successful artist.*

* *I feel happy that I am now surrounded by people who support me and want the best for me.*

* *I feel excited that I am now able to offer people a stable job and that I am making an above-average income.*

* *I feel strong and amazing that I am now in the best physical shape of my life.*

* *I feel at peace now that I am in a healthy, stable romantic relationship.*

* *I feel balanced and centered now that I am meditating and doing yoga every week.*

I have a particular ritual that I use to track my progress with intentions. Each time an intention comes to fruition, I write a *V*, for *victory*, in the corner of the card I've used and pin it up on a corkboard in my home office. Doing this helps my belief system. It also shows me—in black and white—just how powerful I really am.

Exercise: Creating Your Intentions

Get six three-by-five-inch cards. On the unlined side of each card, write one intention using the intention-setting formula. You will use these intention cards during your daily meditation and manifestation routines for Weeks II, III, IV, and beyond.

Take a moment now and read each intention aloud with a voice filled with conviction and confidence.

How did that feel? Did you believe what you just said? Or did that negative voice in your head say, *Oh, give me a break; you're not smart, good, or worthy enough to create these amazing things in your life.*

I thought so.

This is what I lovingly refer to as the "Itty-Bitty Shitty Committee." These are the negative voices that live inside your head that can literally stop you from living the life of your dreams. Before you let them get the best of you, let's meet the little buggers and have a chat. It will help ensure that they do not sabotage your life's new movie.

Director's Notes

- ❊ Read your intentions as part of a ceremony. This is a wonderful way to pull the magic of nature into your world.

- ❊ Rate all of the areas in your life. It can quickly make you aware of what needs to be manifested.

- ❊ Write a *V* for *victory* on each intention as it is realized. Hang each one up, collect them, and realize how powerful you really are.

REPROGRAMMING YOUR BELIEF SYSTEM: CULTIVATING THE POWER TO BELIEVE YOUR DREAMS

"Beyond anything else that we may actually <u>do</u> in our lives, the beliefs that precede our actions are the foundation of all that we cherish, dream, become, and accomplish."

— GREGG BRADEN

It was the day of my scuba-diving certification, and I was about to do the scariest thing I've ever done in my life: submerge myself 60 feet under the surface of the ocean. When I was nine years old, I enjoyed swimming in large bodies of water, as any young girl does. I swam, I splashed, and I played. Then when I was ten, everything changed. I no longer found the idea of the ocean appealing. I only found it horrifying. This new belief—that the ocean was a dark and dangerous place that one should avoid at all costs—came about from my seeing the movie *Jaws*.

In my life movie from then on, I was terrified of sharks and any other sea creature that had the ability to kill me. Going into the water for more than five minutes was not an option for me.

Many years ago, my ex-husband and I owned a beautiful yacht, and when we would go out with friends I was the only one incapable of snorkeling. I would gag every time I put the snorkel in my mouth. I made two of my friends stand on top of the boat on "shark watch" while I dove in for a few minutes with a mask on. If they saw a shark, they were to wave me in.

Of course, that never happened.

Now here I was, about to face one of my greatest fears by getting certified as a scuba diver. Of course, this involved my going into the ocean for prolonged periods of time. I realized I was going to need some help.

I decided to call on one of my practical tools for overcoming fear, called the *character's internal monologue,* which I had first discovered at the water park with my son and had since developed even more. Just before I got into the water, I cued the little make-believe director that lives inside my head. She said to me, *We're rolling, and . . . <u>action!</u>*

I transformed from a woman who believes that the ocean is dangerous and deadly into someone playing a character who is fearless and adventurous, and who believes that the ocean is a magical, beautiful sanctuary. To help me buy into my new belief system, I went one step farther and named the character I was playing Miss Suzy Channing. Suzy, I decided, was a world-class scuba diver.

As I stepped into the role of Suzy, I gracefully put the air regulator into my mouth and began a 60-foot descent into the ocean. Suzy had done this a million times, so it was a piece of cake for her.

My Itty-Bitty Shitty Committee (that internal negative voice) sat in complete silence on the sidelines. In fact, I'd asked one of the movie-crew hands to cleverly tape the Committee's mouths shut so it couldn't say negative things to deter, distract, or deflate me. Fortunately, it wasn't able to play the theme from *Jaws*, either. For now, all was quiet on the set.

I ran Suzy's made-up internal monologue inside my head. This is the same technique I used as an actress. I would not only speak my character's lines, but also think the thoughts that she'd likely think in a given situation. I began to silently say the things a word-class scuba diver would say to herself during a dive like this.

I thought, *This is amazing, and almost as exciting as when I swam with great-white sharks in the Great Barrier Reef! I love my life. And diving is my favorite thing to do. This underwater world is absolutely breathtaking!*

Suddenly, the tool was working. I believed everything I was thinking, and there was no fear.

I was on the ocean floor, still in character as Suzy, and my diving-certification instructor motioned for me to begin my first test: removing my mask and regulator (my only air source), and then putting the mask back on and using an alternative air source. This is a safety skill that we'd practiced the day before in the swimming pool, but now it was the real deal. If I messed up, I could drown.

But no pressure—Suzy had this one. I cued the director in my head once again: *And we are rolling. Action!*

Back in character, I (as Suzy) effortlessly removed my mask and my air source. I put my mask back on. Then I put the other air source in my mouth. I looked at my instructor. He seemed impressed. I certainly was. We went through eight more tests and then ascended to the surface.

When I climbed back on board, everyone applauded. I had done it! The captain took a photo of me in my scuba suit with my thumbs up, which I uploaded to Facebook. My friends and family began to comment on how stunned and proud they were of me.

I gave myself a pat on the back for overcoming a self-limiting belief system that could have kept me out of the beautiful ocean forever . . . if I had let it.

How Do Self-Limiting Negative Belief Systems Work?

A capable hypnotist can convince an entire group of people that they are chickens. The audience roars as a group onstage begins clucking and walking around like barnyard fowl.

The hypnotist has implanted a belief into the subjects' subconscious minds. They believe that they're chickens, even though they're obviously not. They have been programmed and are acting on that belief. My belief system about oceans and sharks worked the same way. I was fearful anytime I was near water, because I had been programmed to think that if I went into the ocean, I would have a good chance of being eaten.

Our negative and limiting belief systems have been deeply imprinted in our subconscious minds, likely from a long time ago. Unfortunately, our culture does an impressive job of implanting things that are simply not accurate. Until we dig deeper and find out what the truth really is, we continue believing what we've been programmed with.

What belief systems have your parents, teachers, or co-workers imprinted onto your subconscious? Who has said that you were not good, smart, or beautiful enough? What false things do you believe about yourself?

Take a moment to tune in to your negative voices. They are the ones that spew out comments about your limitations. They are your Itty-Bitty Shitty Committee.

Well, your Itty-Bitty Shitty Committee is wrong. Its members need to be exposed, stopped, and replaced by your true voice of intuition, which is the one that believes that anything is possible and that your capabilities, in the movie of your life, are limitless.

The Committee was not there when you were born.

Take a moment to think back to preschool or kindergarten. You showed up with a big smile, wearing your favorite purple polka-dot pants. You went about your day fully expressive: singing loudly and finger-painting. There were no voices chiming in to stop you from being the true essence of who you were. There was only your intuitive voice of wisdom, reiterating just how fabulous you were.

And then, something happened as you got a little older. One day someone pointed at your purple polka-dot pants, laughed, and called you a weirdo. Or, as you were happily belting out one of your favorite songs in the car, your mom or dad said, "Stop that awful screeching!" Or perhaps as you painted with complete joy and abandon, a teacher suggested you might want to take up sports, because not everyone can be an artist.

Those jabs at your natural self gave birth to your Committee that's made up of hecklers that live inside your head, voicing all those nasty comments and judgments about you. You may even think that the voices are your own. When the Committee first came on the scene, it was disguised as a group of people trying to pass themselves off as your friends. When you reached for your favorite purple polka-dot pants in the morning, someone on your Committee would sneak in and say, *Oh no, don't wear those pants. Everyone will think you are weird.* When you were about to sing your heart out in chorus, another would say, *Shh. Sing softly so that no one can hear you. You have a terrible singing voice.*

On and on it would go, stopping you from feeling good about who you are and from taking risks. It enjoyed stomping on your bright ideas and inspirations. As you began to grow, the Committee's voice became disguised as your own, and you eventually lost sight of your own wisdom.

The continuation of our work this week is to identify the Committee, understand what negative belief systems have subconsciously been programmed into you, and then begin to reprogram them into positive belief systems. Just as I discovered the limitations that kept me from scuba diving, you must identify what it is that is holding you back, too.

That is how we create the movie of our dreams.

How to Reprogram Negative Belief Systems

How do we reprogram ourselves? How do we love ourselves again after having been told that we are unlovable? Where is the memo telling us that we are powerful creators of our world and not just meant to make the best of the cards we've been dealt? And how do we stop the broken record of thoughts that say, over and over, *You will never succeed?*

In order to move forward, we must reprogram. Our belief systems and our intentions must be in alignment with one another. If they're not, we send out a positive thought grounded in a negative belief.

That, in turn, sends an unclear message to Source, which negates the entire process.

If Source does not receive clear messages, we cannot manifest. If your stated intention is *I am living in a beautiful home in the mountains* and your next thought is *That will never happen,* your intention and your belief are not working in alignment. The belief about your success must be reprogrammed.

To begin doing so, you must first explore your Committee and identify where the voices originated.

Get Curious

My student Donna used curiosity to identify what was limiting her belief system. She came to me one day and said she was preparing to leave her very lucrative job of 25 years as a real-estate agent.

"I know now, after doing this work with you, that I am not living out my life's purpose," she said very softly.

Donna went on to explain that her true love in life was photography. Instead, she was working in a field with no outlet for her creative expression. She felt as if her soul wasn't being honored by the work she was doing. At age 49, she felt that she was wasting her best talents and skills by doing something that was uninspiring. I asked her to show me some of her photography. We turned on my laptop and went to the website she'd created while taking my class.

My jaw dropped.

Not only was the photography unbelievably moving and awe inspiring, but the website was brilliant as well—it had a beautiful color palette and a stunning slide show.

Part of my work as an executive dream producer involves having my creative dream team build websites for my clients. That being said, I am not easily impressed. Looking at what Donna showed me, however, I was more than impressed. After I expressed my appreciation of her work, I asked who had done the graphic work on her website. She said that she'd done it herself. This woman was beyond creative.

I knew immediately that Donna had enormous talent and would be highly successful in the creative field of web design and photography. I looked her directly in the eyes and said, "So what is holding you back from walking out the door?"

"The Itty-Bitty Shitty Committee," she said.

I laughed. "What do they say to you?"

Then she laughed. "You don't want to know."

I told her I did.

"They say things to me like, 'You have no talent, and you are a mediocre photographer who doesn't even know how to use proper professional lighting. You will never earn enough as a photographer to support yourself. You should be grateful to even have a job in this economy. If you leave, you will regret it for the rest of your life, because you are nowhere near good enough to succeed in the competitive field of photography.'"

I nodded. That definitely sounded like the Itty-Bitty Shitty Committee. I then asked, "Where do you think those messages come from? Who might have said things like that to you in the past?"

She didn't hesitate. "My mom. She always said that I wasn't creative. She would dote on my brother and always lavish praise on his artwork. But anytime I would try something artistic, she would look at me and say something like, 'Nice try, honey, but your brother obviously got all the creative talent in this family.'"

"So it sounds as if your mom sits on the Committee," I observed.

She laughed and said, "Actually, I think my mother *runs* the Committee."

"Do you agree with her?" I asked gently.

"No," she said. "I think I am very talented. But I never really stopped and got curious about who was on the Committee. I never thought about who was saying all of that negative stuff to me."

I lit up. She had just said the magic word: *curious.* The best antidote to judgment is curiosity.

When we start inquiring about the negative voices beating us up, they're suddenly silenced. Our inner dialogue changes in profound ways. Just by identifying where these voices originate, we have the power to switch them off.

After all, they're someone else's judgments. They are not our own. And since they aren't true, we don't have to own them—or believe them. They are another person's belief systems.

Before I learned more about quantum physics, I didn't understand that I was part of Source. As a result, I also didn't have the power to communicate with this powerful energy field. Back when I was the star of *One Hot Mess,* I had no idea that everything I thought, believed, and felt was creating my reality. Discovering quantum physics changed all of that for me.

I mentioned Lynne McTaggart's *Living the Field* and Gregg Braden's *The Divine Matrix* in the Introduction. These two books make it easy to understand quantum physics and are wonderful introductions to this amazing new world.

The "Meet Your Committee" Exercise

You will need a blank piece of paper and a pen or colored markers for this exercise:

1. Think about the negative self-talk that goes on in your head. Perhaps there is negative talk about your health, your lack of follow-through, or your inability to succeed in your career. Many people have voices that say they aren't good enough, don't deserve and will never find love, or are too old to try something new. Others have voices that say they are fat, not educated enough, or not creative enough to live their dreams. Now, imagine that there are three nasty characters responsible for bringing all the negativity into your life.

2. Draw those three Committee members. (Don't let them convince you that you can't draw!)

3. Name your three Committee members, using the first three names that pop into your head.

4. In a talk bubble above each member's head, write one thing that they say to you.

For example, my Committee is composed of:

The *New York Times* critic: No one is going to read your book! It's all been said before. You have nothing original to say. Give up now, before you make a fool of yourself.

Miss Perfect: You need to lose ten more pounds. You are getting wrinkles on the sides of your mouth. Do not even think about leaving the house without a padded push-up bra!

Nasty Nancy: You are not enough—not smart enough, not tall enough, not creative enough, not rich enough, not thin enough, not focused enough, and not balanced enough.

For the next week, hang up your drawings in a place where you will see them every day. They'll be a reminder to stay in observation mode and note what your Committee is saying about you.

During this time, simply notice what they say. Make a note of how they try to put you down or stop you from taking risks. Whenever they come up with an obnoxious comment, call them out by name. Tell them that no one will listen to them anymore. Replace their nasty comments with compassionate ones.

When you confront your Committee, it's a reminder that *they* are not *you*. That, in turn, automatically defuses their power.

Once you realize that your Committee isn't telling you the truth and that others have implanted your negative belief systems in your mind, you can begin reprogramming those beliefs. You can make them align with your intentions and make your movie come to life.

Beliefs vs. Facts

A *fact* is a verifiable truth. A *belief* is what someone has decided is the truth. It may or may not be verifiable. But a fact is a fact and cannot be changed. You can, however, always choose what you believe. It doesn't matter how long you've held on to a belief or where it came from. You can adopt a new one whenever you choose.

When I was single, I wasn't in a relationship. That's an easily verifiable fact. During my retreat in Bali, I decided that I wanted to find a romantic partner. To make that wish a reality, I had to adopt a new belief system that would support me in finding a new love.

As I reentered the dating world, I paid close attention to the belief systems that many single women hold. I heard them saying, "There are no good men" or "Men only want to date 20-year-olds." That was what Source tuned in to for them. That's also what happened in their lives. Because of their negative expectations, they were on a path filled with the men they believed weren't available to them.

I chose a different belief system. I went with a more positive outlook: there are plenty of men available to me, and my next partner is on the way.

My friends who chose the negative thoughts are still single. But within 30 days of my adopting my own positive system, I met the perfect new man.

Here are a few examples of facts, and the negative and positive belief systems we can choose to change or perpetuate.

Fact	Negative Belief	Positive Belief
I'm single.	*It's because I'm unlovable.*	*My partner is on the way!*
I have $450.	*I am a failure.*	*I can rebuild my wealth!*
I'm not fulfilled at work.	*I hate my job.*	*I will find my dream job!*

Your Itty-Bitty Shitty Committee is constantly delivering negative beliefs. Your job is to replace their voices with something positive!

Replacing Negative Beliefs with Positive Beliefs

There are many ways to leave your negative beliefs behind. You can refocus on positive outcomes by using hypnosis, working with a therapist, or using positive affirmations.

Affirmations are the cheapest method I know. They are a wonderful way to reprogram negative thought patterns into positive ones. We must rebuild our belief systems into ones that support us, rather than hold us back. This is an essential part of creating the movie of our new lives.

Reading daily affirmations during your meditation and manifestation routine will reprogram what no longer serves you. It will also enable you to work with the Law of Attraction, as you need to believe your intentions in order for the Law of Attraction to work in your favor.

People with a history of abuse (mental, physical, or sexual) tend to carry around particularly damaging negative belief systems. These folks are best served by repeating affirmations multiple times each day. I also suggest working with a therapist or bodyworker to overcome the particularly loud Itty-Bitty Shitty Committee created by trauma.

You will know when your affirmations begin to work. You'll find yourself feeling more open, relaxed, and confident. You will begin to see your intentions manifest, and the shouting done by your Itty-Bitty Shitty Committee will be reduced to whispers.

Daily Affirmations Exercise: Creating Six Powerful Affirmations

1. Pick six affirmations from the following lists that I've provided, or make up your own.

2. On the unlined side of a different three-by-five-inch card from the one you have written down your intentions, write one affirmation.

3. Repeat this step for the five remaining affirmations you have chosen on five other cards.

Affirmations for Prosperity and Abundance

✳ *I always have more than enough to share with others.*

✳ *I have opened the floodgates of abundance and prosperity.*

✳ *The universe is always conspiring with me and often surprises me with blessings.*

✳ *I am surrounded by people who need what I have to offer.*

✳ *I exude power, purpose, and prosperity everywhere I go.*

✳ *I am a magnet for opportunity and success.*

✳ *My intuition leads me to create opportunity.*

✳ *I have expanded my awareness to the hidden potential in every situation.*

✳ *Money flows to me effortlessly.*

✳ *My income is constantly increasing.*

Affirmations for Positive Health and Body Image

✳ *My health and well-being are my top priority.*

✳ *Every cell in my body is beaming with energy and light.*

✳ *I love the way I feel.*

✳ *My flaws are transformed by self-love and self-acceptance.*

✳ *I honor my body, strength, and uniqueness.*

✳ *I am free of pain and suffering.*

✳ *I take time to meditate and listen to my body.*

✳ *I feel balanced, healthy, and whole.*

✳ *I have unlimited amounts of energy and vitality.*

✳ *I am proud of my strong and powerful body.*

Affirmations for Self-Confidence and Self-Belief

✻ *I transform my life by changing my beliefs.*

✻ *My willpower is stronger than my bad habits.*

✻ *Fear is a temporary feeling.*

✻ *I have the willpower to try, and I will be successful.*

✻ *I am willing to fail in order to succeed.*

✻ *I am confident and like who I am.*

✻ *I believe I have the power to create my world.*

✻ *I am intelligent and have important things to communicate.*

✻ *I feel comfortable in my own skin.*

✻ *I know I have the power to be anything I want to be.*

Life's Purpose Affirmations

✻ *The better I get to know myself, the clearer my purpose becomes.*

✻ *I am limited only by my perception of what is possible.*

✻ *I am meant to do great things that touch the lives of others.*

✻ *When I partake in the things that fascinate me, I live out my life's purpose.*

✻ *I know what my greatest gifts and talents are.*

✻ *I am fully expressed in who I am.*

✻ *I make a difference in the lives of others by being in touch with who I am.*

✻ *I share my knowledge with others and express my life's purpose through communicating who I am.*

✻ *I do what I love and love what I do.*

✻ *I create abundance when I tap into my greatest gifts and talents, and share them with others.*

Affirmations for Love

❋ *I am a being of pure love.*

❋ *I love and accept myself exactly as I am.*

❋ *I deserve love.*

❋ *I am in a healthy, conscious relationship where love, friendship, and abundance flow in equal measures.*

❋ *It is easy for me to express love, and in return it is easily expressed back to me.*

❋ *Each day, more love fills my life.*

❋ *I love myself and others unconditionally.*

❋ *Each day, there is more love and happiness in all of my relationships.*

❋ *I am patient and kind, and I freely give my love.*

❋ *I naturally attract loving, fun relationships.*

Affirmations for Clarity

❋ *I trust my feelings and insights.*

❋ *I am detached from outcome and open to my inner guidance.*

❋ *I have awakened to a higher wisdom.*

❋ *I am clear about my life's purpose.*

❋ *I am clear about what a conscious relationship looks like.*

❋ *I am clear about what I want to manifest into my life.*

❋ *I am clear because I take time to meditate.*

❋ *I am clear about how to keep my body, mind, and spirit in perfect balance.*

❋ *I take time to organize my life.*

❋ *I listen to my intuition, and it guides me well.*

Practicing Affirmations

Take a moment now to practice. Get your six cards out, and ask your Committee to kindly leave the room!

Now, read each affirmation. Read it aloud in a voice of powerful conviction and confidence. (This practice will be added to your daily meditation and manifestation routine.)

Sit at your meditation station and silently read all six affirmation cards to help put you in a positive state of believing. Then, read each card aloud.

Before reading your affirmations, you may also find it helpful to say two statements about yourself that are currently true, such as:

I am [write your name]. *I am from* [city, state].

This allows you to begin the session with two statements that you can say with complete confidence. After making these declarations, read your affirmations in the exact same voice and with the same cadence.

This technique will help tap into your ability to make statements with complete conviction. If you falter or do not feel confident, go back and repeat what you know to be true. Then, return to the affirmations and intentions. When you've reprogrammed your belief system with the first six affirmations, pick six new ones. As you might imagine, this technique of reading the affirmations aloud is also a helpful way for you to believe in your intentions. Try this technique with your intention cards as well.

Your Itty-Bitty Shitty Committee may have had a very powerful hold on you for a very long time. This is really okay, for no matter how powerful, all-encompassing, intimidating, persistent, unforgiving, unflappable, unflinching, and unkind your Committee may have been to you, you have something that it will never be able to conquer: the belief that you can live the life of your dreams.

Director's Notes

※ Using the actor's tool of running a positive internal monologue in your head will help you conquer things that scare you.

※ Using curiosity as the antidote to judgment is a great way to understand the origin of the Itty-Bitty Shitty Committee's negative beliefs.

※ Naming and drawing your Committee is a good way to differentiate yourself from it and to realize that its voices are not yours.

※ Affirmations are a great way to reprogram your limiting belief systems.

Soulwork: Week II

Please do the following for the next seven days:

※ Write your name on one three-by-five-inch card (I am Jennifer Grace).

※ Write where you were born on one three-by-five-inch card (I am from Brooklyn, New York).

※ Write six different intentions, each one on a different three-by-five-inch card (positive thoughts).

※ Write six different affirmations, each one on a different three-by-five-inch card (positive beliefs).

In order to become the producer of your life, get curious about the origin of your negative and limiting belief systems. Where did they come from? Who once said these things to you? Remember to notice your Committee all week and mute what it says. Then use these journal prompts to find the origin of your belief systems:

※ *My belief about money is . . .*

※ *My belief about love is . . .*

※ *My belief about health is . . .*

※ *My belief about power is . . .*

※ *My belief about my purpose is . . .*

※ *My belief about myself is . . .*

※ *My belief about my ability to succeed is . . .*

Each day, journal in a stream-of-consciousness fashion for five minutes, using one journal prompt each day.

Week II: Daily Meditation and Manifestation Routine

Below is the Week II daily meditation and manifestation routine. You should be sitting up with your spine straight for this meditation. You may want to have someone read it to you, or simply record it for yourself. You can also download a free MP3 of the routine from my website at **www.thecenterofgrace.com/meditation**.

Begin by using the Five-Senses Check-In to create a state of balance, clarity, and focus.

First, evoke the sense of sight. Look around the room. Notice the colors and textures. Move your eyes from object to object. If you notice a thought about the past or the future, simply move your gaze to the next object in the room. Notice anything in the room that you've never noticed before. What do you see?

Now, close your eyes and evoke the sense of smell. Breathe in deeply. Notice if you smell anything specific in the room. It could be something you cooked earlier, the scent of a candle, or a breeze coming through the window.

Next, evoke the sense of sound. Notice sounds inside the room. Then notice sounds coming from outside. Try listening with just your right ear and then your left.

Now, evoke the sense of touch. Notice how your feet feel on the floor. Then notice how your clothing feels on your body and how the air feels on your cheek.

Finally, evoke the sense of taste. Gently glide your tongue along the top of your teeth, and swallow.

Now just be.

Open your eyes and return to the room. Be here now.

Next, begin the manifestation portion of your daily routine. Have your six affirmation cards and your six intention cards ready. Start with affirmations. Read each card either aloud or silently to yourself. As you read, lift your heart and infuse yourself with confidence and knowing. Next, do the same with your intentions, also reading them silently or aloud. As you read each card, again lift your heart and infuse yourself with confidence and knowing. Your work is done.

Your intentions have been set.

Begin your ten-minute meditation session by taking in three long, deep breaths. Straighten your spine and rest your hands lightly on your thighs.

Begin to follow your breath in and out. When a thought comes in, simply notice it. Do not label it as <u>good</u> or <u>bad</u>. Just say <u>Thinking</u> and return to your breath. You may want to use a mantra as you meditate. Say <u>in</u> on the inhalation, and <u>out</u> on the exhalation. Or try <u>here</u> on the in breath, and <u>now</u> on the out breath.

(Sit quietly for ten minutes of silent meditation.)

You have now completed your daily meditation and manifestation routine.

BECOMING THE PRODUCER OF YOUR DREAMS,

continued

Tools Needed for Week III:

- Your six completed three-by-five-inch intention cards
- Some blank sheets of paper and a pen

Practice 6

AUTHENTICALLY ACTING AS IF: CULTIVATING TRUTHFUL EMOTIONS TO FEEL YOUR DREAMS

"[W]e don't live for the realities but for the fantasies, the dreams of what might be. If we lived for reality, we'd be dead, every last one of us. Only dreams keep us going."

— MICHAEL SHURTLEFF

In junior high school, my best friend Amy and I would create music videos in our minds while listening to love songs. We dreamed about dates with boys and devised soundtracks to accompany our fantasy lives. They didn't all come true, but they were the beginning of a practice I've used ever since.

At first, I didn't realize that listening to uplifting music during my manifestation sessions was a repeat of something that I'd already learned as a teenager. I also didn't consciously realize that I was using my acting techniques to create the emotional resonance of my dream life. I was doing it all unconsciously, but I was communicating with Source nonetheless.

One day, after a Manifesting 101 workshop, my student Jeanette approached me. Jeanette understood from my lecture that thinking, believing, and *feeling* the intent behind our goals is important when communicating our dreams to Source, but she was still having issues.

She said, "Jen, I'm doing everything you're teaching me. I journal and meditate, and I read my intentions and affirmations on a daily basis. But I still don't understand how to *feel* what I'm intending. Do you have a tool you can give me to feel it? Your system is working for you, so let me in on your secret. What do you do that you aren't telling me about?"

I honestly wasn't aware of any special trick that I'd been using, but promised I would observe myself and report back what I discovered.

I awoke the next morning feeling mildly anxious, likely because the previous evening my accountant informed me that I owed quite a bit in taxes. I had just started earning an income after becoming self-employed and had not budgeted for this unwelcome news. I was slightly panicked.

I had no desire to manifest or meditate that morning. I felt nervous. It didn't seem like the right time to read cards filled with optimistic intentions. All I wanted to do was sulk and feel sorry for myself.

Out of nowhere, I heard the words of my former theater director, Kim St. Leon: "Kid, take your crap and put it on the shelf. It will still be there when all this is over. The show must go on."

It was the advice that had gotten me through many performances. So I sat down at my meditation station and picked up my cards.

The first card said, "I am overjoyed that I am creating unlimited abundance while doing what I love."

I read it aloud, but my voice didn't sound overjoyed at all. It was downright scared; I was facing a tax bill that might result in my having to get a real job, after all. How could I feel overjoyed about that?

"The show must go on," I heard Kim say again.

I sat up straight. I closed my eyes and opened them again. Then I reached over to my laptop and started playing "Primavera," a song that always puts me in a better mood. In fact, I play it often during my manifestation sessions to help shift my mood.

I closed my eyes and listened. Suddenly, I was catapulted back to my days as a commercial actress for an orange-juice company. I had unexpectedly received a residual check for $35,000 out of nowhere one day, which caused me to jump for joy! The memory of that moment even got me through a number of later scenes when I had to be excited and overjoyed onstage or on set.

I revisited that time once more, and then opened my eyes. I read my intention card again. This time, joy flowed through me. I was no longer anxious or afraid. I sincerely felt elation and confidence.

I closed my eyes once more and envisioned a solution that would rescue me from my tax troubles. I was running a *mind movie.* My closed eyelids were a movie screen, and my imagination was a projector. I was showing myself the future experience I desired, just as I had done as a teenager.

I saw myself filled with gratitude and abundance for this future solution. I let excitement bubble up within me, and I was relieved and happy in the movie I was seeing. It was all in perfect sync with the music playing in the background.

My entire body was covered with goose bumps.

Just then, my phone rang. It was my accountant, who had spoken to my ex-husband. He had forgotten to write off some expense, and as a result, I would not have to pay any taxes after all. Even better, I would receive a refund of nearly $5,000!

My entire body was covered with goose bumps again. What an unexpected surprise.

That's when I realized the secret I hadn't shared with my students. (Of course, I didn't realize it was a secret at all.) I'd been unconsciously using the actor's tool of substitution. It allowed me to tap into a memory and capture an authentic emotion. I was also scripting scenes I wanted to experience in my life, the same way I used to script scenes when I was a screenwriter.

Immediately, I called up Jeanette and expressed my gratitude. She had pushed me to uncover this secret. I knew from her enthusiasm that I was onto something.

That spark of insight was a huge breakthrough in my work as a transformational teacher. I was now able to use my training as an actor and screenwriter to help students access the emotions necessary for manifesting their future lives.

That is the secret at the heart of this book, too. While nearly all the material that's available about manifestation highlights the need to communicate your emotions to Source, most don't actually provide a practical method for doing so. In this practice, I'll do just that.

Acting, Not "Smachting"

I trained to be an actress in the Conservatory Training Program at The Acting Studio in Hollywood, Florida. There, I learned myriad techniques from legendary acting teachers. Through their instruction, I also gathered a number of tools that would help me beyond my time on the stage. There was a powerful common denominator underlying everything I learned.

"Jen, you're *smachting*, not acting. Do it again," my teacher Michael Joya would say.

Smachting meant faking it. If you weren't feeling the true emotional life of a character, you were smachting. When this happened, I'd stop and reach for a tool to access that truth. This wasn't easy, but it worked.

The best actors, of course, make it look easy. That's why they're the best. Meryl Streep and Daniel Day-Lewis make acting appear seamless. It's often difficult to know where they end and their characters begin. You *believe* them as you watch them on-screen. In fact, they're so good that they make you feel the emotions of their characters, too.

There's an enormous amount of effort behind those seamless performances. Actors study life, enliven their senses, and infuse themselves with their characters' emotions.

To prepare for a role, actors use a process called "acting as if." They conjure up true feelings that will be believable to audiences and themselves. The process includes many different exercises and requires a lot of skillful imagination. The goal is to live the emotional life of the character.

The same concept applies to manifesting. To properly do so, we must believe in something that hasn't actually happened. We have to feel as if it has.

Using the same tool employed by actors, you can believe in something that hasn't yet happened. I use four exercises in my workshop titled Authentically Acting as If, and you can incorporate these into your own practices, too.

If you're feeling sad, anxious, or depressed, it can seem impossible to access the emotions of joy, love, and abundance. But if you overcome that feeling of impossibility for just 15 minutes during your daily manifestation routine, it can make all the difference in the world.

In short, you have to "put your crap on the shelf" for a few minutes every day. It will still be there when you're done, but the manifestation show must go on.

The Four AFM™ Exercises and Cultivating Your Imagination

Actors constantly live inside their own heads. After all, it's the world of imagination that allows them to create rich, believable experiences onstage. To be truthful in their roles, they must access past memories.

As the writer, producer, and director of your own life movie, you must do the same. You can do just that by using the four exercises that follow. I call them the Authentic Frequency Method (AFM). Each of these tools will help you imagine and authentically feel the life you are trying to manifest.

Authentic Frequency Acting
Exercise: Screenwriting Your Future-Life Script

You can't act if you don't have a script, so the first step toward acting "as if" is to develop a future-life script so that you have a role to authentically portray.

A future-life script is a scene you write from your very own imagination that you'd like to star in. This is where you begin to create your future life from nothing.

To do this, pull out your six intention cards (the ones you created during Practice 4). Then, write one of those intentions on the top of a blank sheet of paper. (You can do the other five intentions during your Week III Soulwork.)

Write the script of a future scene that brings this intention to life. Add as many details as possible to make yours vivid and believable. Use your imagination.

Begin by imagining what if this intention were already real. Doing so will keep your Committee silent and allow your imagination to take over.

Here is my own future-life script for one of my long-term intentions:

Intention: I am overjoyed that I am spending time at my beautiful second home in Boulder, Colorado. I love being surrounded by the lake and the mountains.

Magic what if: What if I somehow acquired enough money to own a second home in Colorado?

Location: Boulder, Colorado

Wardrobe: A cozy, cream-colored robe

Season: Fall

Time of day: 3:00 P.M.

Set: Large living room with a couch, coffee table, fireplace, big bay windows, and a soft shag rug

Props: Tea set, book, and cream-colored slippers by the side of the couch

Aromas: Jasmine-and-mint tea

Sounds: Crackle of fire, birds, wind in the trees

Soundtrack: "Sunrise" by Norah Jones

Emotional state: Content and accomplished

Scene: I am wearing my plush cream-colored robe and sitting on a cozy couch in my living room. The couch is brown crushed velvet; it is so soft that my body sinks into it, holding me gently in its arms. There is a coffee table in front of me. A beautiful baby-blue-and-chocolate-brown tea set sits on it. I smell the jasmine and mint tea as it steeps in my cup. The fire in the fireplace makes snapping and crackling sounds. It's not that cold outside, since it's October, but I want the fire going anyway. I am reading a book. Every so often, I look up and out of my large bay windows. I stare in wonder at the beautiful fall colors. I feel a deep level of contentment and accomplishment. The lake outside beckons, and I know that after this chapter, I will take my yellow kayak out for a row. I happily anticipate my guests, who will

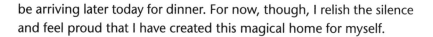
be arriving later today for dinner. For now, though, I relish the silence and feel proud that I have created this magical home for myself.

This is my scene, filled with my own passions and intentions. In this case, the details are aligned with my own sense of my future self. Even though I could choose many ways to write about my Colorado home, these are the details that speak to me and ignite my passions. I feel an authentic, emotional truth in my script.

Your own script should have that same personal detail. It doesn't matter what kind of scene you write. It only matters that it's a true reflection of your intention and what you desire. Be playful, have fun, and let your imagination soar.

Authentic Frequency Acting Exercise: Memory Script

We perceive the world through our senses. We see, hear, smell, touch, and taste, and our senses stimulate us. The recollection of what we experienced can also impact us in powerful ways. We've all felt hungry and salivated at the thought of a favorite food or heard a song that takes us back to a past relationship. Our memories are strongly linked to our senses. Through practice, we can learn to use those sensory memories to connect with our future-life situations, which causes our intentions to come to life. We can experience true emotion through our sensory connection to a particular person, place, or time from our past.

Once your future-life script is complete, make note of the emotions running through it. How will you feel when this comes true? In my script, contentment and accomplishment are at the center of my scene.

If I were an actor playing this part at a time when my personal life seemed like a failure, I would access a memory of a similar accomplishment—a college graduation, for example—and substitute that sense of success for my own feelings of failure.

Actors frequently use this technique when preparing for a role. Old flames are substituted for costars in a love scene, for example, in a quest to feel authentically in love. Using memories will help you experience honest emotions as you manifest your future life. It will infuse the scenes you are manifesting with authenticity and believability, for your memories will stimulate your senses in a similar way to how they did when the event you are remembering actually took place.

Here is my life-memory script for contentment and accomplishment:

Emotional state of character: Contentment and Accomplishment

Memory to conjure up emotional state: The day I graduated college

Location: Tucson, Arizona

Wardrobe: Blue graduation gown and hat

Season: Late spring

Time of day: 2:00 P.M.

Set: Large outdoor stadium, stage, audience

Props: Podium and diploma

Aromas: Cactus blooming

Sounds: Applause

Memory scene: I am walking onto the stage to receive my diploma. I can feel my blue robe swish lightly around my ankles. It is warm under the hot Arizona sun, and I smell cactus blossoms in the air. Then, I hear my name called. My heart flutters with excitement as I walk to the podium. I see the crowd. Thousands of people are watching me. I see the pride in my parents' eyes. I see all of my friends in the audience. I was the only one out of all my friends to graduate in four years. I did it!

Now you try. Choose a memory related to the emotional state in your future-life script. For example, if you want to bring love into your life, choose a memory related to a past loving experience. If your goal is to have better health, focus on a particular memory of when you felt vital and healthy. It's important that your memory script be specific and related to a key emotion from your future-life script.

You may have noticed that I wrote the scene in the present tense, not the past tense. Writing in the present tense will help you relate to the memory, not as something from a different time, but as authentic emotions you feel in the present moment.

Authentic Frequency Acting Exercise: Using Substitution

Use the substitution meditation that follows to guide you in experiencing this memory script. Then substitute the emotion you felt back then into your future-life script. It will authentically bring the emotions that you'll need in order to communicate with Source.

This is the guided Substitution Meditation in written form. You may want to have someone read it to you, or you may want to record it yourself. You can also download a free MP3 version from my website: **www.thecenterofgrace.com/meditation.**

Substitution Meditation

This meditation will guide you on a journey from the past to the future.

First, read one of your future-life scripts. Do this to tune in to the emotional state you need in order to conjure up a memory in which this emotion was present. This memory will help you infuse your future life with authentic emotion.

Now, find a quiet place to lie down. Gently close your eyes.

Take several long, deep breaths. You have nowhere to go and nowhere to be except right here, right now.

Imagine that you are walking down a softly lit corridor. At the end is a bright-green door. This is the door that will lead you to your memory.

You arrive at the door and gently open it, walking into a scene from your past.

Look around. Where are you? Who is with you? What color are the walls? What type of furniture is in the room?

What sounds do you hear? Are people talking? What are they saying?

Breathe in. What smells are in the air?

You see a mirror and walk over to it. Your reflection stares back, and you notice your age and what you are wearing that day. You smile at yourself. Today is a very good day.

You turn away from the mirror, and the scene from your past begins to unfold. You start to feel the rush of emotion that you felt on that day. Whether it was love, abundance, vitality, peace, or joy, this feeling begins in your toes and runs all the way up your body. It plants a big smile on your face. You play out this memory in your mind. You feel and experience everything from that past day.

The scene begins to come to an end. You suddenly see another door. This one is bright yellow.

You gently open the door and walk from your past into your future.

Look around. Where are you? Who is there with you? What color are the walls? What type of furniture is in the room?

Now listen. What sounds do you hear? Are people talking? What are they saying?

Breathe in. What smells are in the air?

You see a mirror and walk over to it. Your reflection stares back at you, and you notice your age and what you are wearing. You smile at yourself. Today is a very good day.

You turn away from the mirror. Your future-life script begins to unfold.

As you master this practice, you will soon realize that you no longer need to relive the entire memory. You will immediately fast-forward to the elated feeling of the memory, and effortlessly transfer it to your future intention. All it takes is practice.

How to Use Future-Life and Memory Scripts

Incorporate your scripts into your daily manifestation and meditation routine. Once your future-life script has been written, run it as a mind movie before you meditate. If you need help accessing an emotional state for your script, use a memory to help. Once you have created all six life scripts, as defined by your six intentions, focus on one mind movie each day.

You can also select music for your mind movie. Music can instantly lift your emotions. It can also play a powerful role in your manifestation work.

You can create a soundtrack for your future life that includes different songs for different emotional states. For example, I play Mozart when I want to access peace, Whitney Houston's "I'm Every Woman"

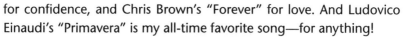
for confidence, and Chris Brown's "Forever" for love. And Ludovico Einaudi's "Primavera" is my all-time favorite song—for anything!

Once you've selected your songs, copy them onto a CD or create a playlist for your MP3 player. Play it in your car or while on a run to help you access the appropriate emotional states for your manifestations.

Authentic Frequency Acting Exercise: Improvisation

My workshops include an improvisational game I call "The Cocktail Party." I pass out cocktail glasses and name tags to my students. Then, I ask them to write three things about themselves on their name tags, and all three items must be related to their future selves.

Then, everyone acts as if they were at a cocktail party, chatting and mingling with other guests. The cocktail party is five years in the future. Guests are living their future lives. They are not allowed to break character. Everyone must be their future selves. (This is exactly the game I was playing on the yacht with my friend Pamela.)

This is a great exercise to try with friends. Have your own cocktail party and ask everyone to bring their future selves. Or, invite one friend to lunch. Role-play throughout the entire meal, and catch up about your amazing new lives!

Director's Notes

- ✳ Creating future-life scripts helps you write the story of your life.
- ✳ Finding past emotional memories helps you authentically communicate that emotion to Source as you manifest the life of your dreams.
- ✳ Creating a soundtrack for your future life helps you tap into your desired emotional state through the power of music.

Soulwork: Week III

- ✳ Write one future-life script each day for one of your six intentions.

✳ Write one memory script each day that conjures up the key emotional state present in your intentions.

Week III: Daily Meditation and Manifestation Routine

This is the written Week III daily meditation routine. You should be sitting up with your spine straight for this meditation. You may want to have someone read it to you, or you may want to record it yourself. You can also download a free MP3 version from my website at **www.thecenterofgrace.com/meditation**.

Begin by using the Five-Senses Check-In to create a state of balance, clarity, and focus. First, evoke the sense of sight. Look around the room. Notice the colors and textures. Move your eyes from object to object. If you notice a thought about the past or the future, simply move your gaze to the next object in the room. Notice anything in the room that you've never noticed before. What do you see?

Now, close your eyes and evoke the sense of smell. Breathe in deeply. Notice if you smell anything specific in the room. It could be something you cooked earlier, the scent of a candle, or a breeze coming through the window.

Next, evoke the sense of sound. Notice sounds inside the room. Then notice sounds coming from outside. Try listening with just your right ear and then your left.

Now, evoke the sense of touch. Notice how your feet feel on the floor. Then notice how your clothing feels on your body and how the air feels on your cheek.

Finally, evoke the sense of taste. Gently glide your tongue along the top of your teeth, and swallow.

Now just be.

Open your eyes and return to the room. Be here now.

Next, begin the manifestation portion of your daily routine. Have your six affirmation cards and your six intention cards ready. Start with affirmations. Read each card either aloud or silently to yourself. As you read, lift your heart and infuse yourself with confidence and knowing. Now do the same with your intentions, also reading them silently or aloud. As you read each card, again lift your heart and infuse yourself with confidence and knowing.

Close your eyes and imagine your intentions becoming reality. Envision your future life memory. As you visualize each of your scripted scenes, allow the music to move and assist you in matching your energetic frequency with the emotions connected to your manifestation.

Evoke all five senses until the movie feels real and true. Remember, you are the director of your destiny and the creator of your dreams. See it happening. Feel it becoming reality.

You are powerful beyond measure. This is your life and your movie. You get to decide how it ends.

Your work is done. Your intentions have been set. Commune in silence.

Begin your ten-minute meditation session by taking in three long, deep breaths. Straighten your spine and rest your hands lightly on your thighs.

Begin to follow your breath in and out. When a thought comes in, simply notice it. Do not label it as good or bad. Just say Thinking and return to your breath. You may want to use a mantra as you meditate. Say in on the inhalation and out on the exhalation. Or try here on the in breath and now on the out breath.

(Sit quietly for ten minutes of silent meditation.)

You have now completed your daily meditation and manifestation routine.

BECOMING THE DIRECTOR OF YOUR DREAMS

Tools Needed for Week IV:

❋ *Your three-by-five-inch intention cards*

According to Wikipedia, film directors "are responsible for overseeing creative aspects of a film. They often develop the vision for a film and carry out the vision, deciding how the film should look; in other words, they make their vision come to life."

That definition makes me smile. There are so many similarities between a manifester and a film director. The point of this book is to help you create a vision, too. That has been the focus of our first three weeks. The Law of Attention practices in Week I helped to clarify your vision.

The Law of Attraction practices in Weeks II and III helped you to ensure that your thoughts, beliefs, and emotions were in positive alignment.

Now, during Week IV we must learn to work with the Law of Action. This is when the vision we have created is put into motion.

Working with the Law of Action involves using the two catch-phrases of every film director: *Action,* which is about bringing the vision to life, and *Cut,* which is when we surrender the details to Source.

You must put action behind your newfound thoughts and beliefs in order to create your new reality. That is how you begin directing your destiny.

No director, of course, can complete a film on his or her own; nor can we manifest without support. It is important to have allies who can help us execute our vision.

Will and Grace

There are usually two assistant directors who help to make each film. The first assistant director (or 1st AD) is the director's right-hand person. This individual is responsible for many of the on-set details, allowing the director to focus on the creative process. He or she must have impeccable organizational and time-management skills, the vision to plan ahead, as well as the ability to be a great troubleshooter. This role also demands the willingness to put in the hours required to get the job done.

The second assistant director (or 2nd AD) is the left-hand person. He or she is the person charged with making sure that actors are in the right place at the right time. The 2nd AD also handles any unresolved details, which likewise frees up the director to work at his or her maximum creative capacity.

The director, then, is an eagle with two wings that act as guides: the 1st AD on the right, and the 2nd AD on the left. This perfect balance allows the film to reach its highest potential.

You, too, will need two assistant directors. I call them Will and Grace—and they aren't just a really wonderful '90s television series.

Will, your 1st AD, represents the deliberate steps necessary for you to realize your dreams and oversee tasks such as organization, time management, and action planning.

Your 2nd AD, Grace, represents the serendipitous coincidences that occur when you surrender to Source. When you learn to do this, Source delivers the right actors at just the right times.

Many people are only working with Will. They are very driven merely by action to get what they want. Although they often succeed, they do so at a high cost. Sometimes, it comes in the form of a heart attack. Other times, it manifests as a divorce. In every case, these directors are only using one wing. Just like a bird that only flaps one wing, they go around in circles, never reaching their highest potential.

Other people only live in Grace. These are the individuals who make beautiful vision boards and then wait for their dreams to magically materialize. They are in a state of complete surrender.

In order for our dreams to manifest, we need the "Will" to get up off the couch, and the "Grace" to allow Source to codirect our movies with us. Nothing happens without action and surrender.

The book you are now reading is a direct result of the coordinated work of Will and Grace. In fact, this book was literally manifested. It all happened with the help of Will, Grace, and the Law of Action.

Will arrived on my movie set first. He was responding to my 2010 intention to become a published author. *OK, Jen,* he said. *If you want to be published, you have to actually write a book.*

Well, I know that, Will, I said incredulously. *But how am I going to find the time to write a book? I have an 11-year-old son and no after-school care. I teach classes all over the state, and I have a dozen or more clients to coach each week.*

Will looked at me with a devilish grin. *You will never find the time,* he said. *You have to create the time.*

But there is no time, I argued.

Then you don't want it badly enough.

I sulked for two days. Then it hit me. What do athletes do when they're training for a difficult challenge or event? They wake up early!

I quickly did the math: I would wake up at 5:30 A.M., write for an hour, and still have 30 minutes to do my daily meditation and manifestation routine. I'd be finished with everything by the time my son woke up at 7:00 each morning. That way, I'd have an hour of writing time each day.

I thought I could write about 500 words an hour and would need 50,000 words for a book. That meant I could finish my first draft in 100 days. Perfect!

So I set my alarm for 5:30, and when it went off the next morning, I hit SNOOZE . . . a few times . . . until 6:30, actually.

I was deflated. How could I overcome the self-sabotaging urge to sleep, ignoring my goal to be an author?

Then I remembered what Will said to me: *I guess you don't want it badly enough.*

But I did! The next night, I decided to outwit myself. Instead of just setting my alarm, I also programmed a reminder on my phone. At 5:30, a message would pop up.

"Jen, do you want it, or not?" it would ask me.

I knew that if I was confronted with that challenge every morning, I would be inspired to get out of bed and write. Sure enough, I was up at 5:30 the next morning. I wrote—with a little help from Will—nearly every day for four months. I was able to reach my 50,000-word goal.

Then, Grace arrived on the set.

It was January 2011. I was leading a retreat in Sedona, Arizona. My business partner and I signed up 18 people. We were going to hold a manifestation ceremony in Boynton Canyon on the Kachina Woman rock formation, which is the site of a very powerful vortex.

At this time, I had just finished my first draft of *Directing Your Destiny*. That day, I went to the mountaintop and asked Source to help me accomplish a major challenge.

"I want to be a published Hay House author," I said.

I had no idea how this was going to happen, but I made the request with every ounce of power and conviction inside of me. I said my intention aloud: "I feel ecstatic that I am now a Hay House published author."

I closed my eyes and ran a mind movie. In that movie was a circle of other Hay House authors, all holding hands. Wayne Dyer, Louise Hay, Cheryl Richardson, Gregg Braden, Doreen Virtue, and Christiane Northrup were all there. I walked over to them. Louise and Wayne turned their heads toward me, parted their hands, and welcomed me into their circle.

The feeling was so real that I could feel Louise squeeze my right hand.

When I returned from Sedona, I called my ex-husband and recounted my mountaintop experience.

"Now all I need is for Wayne Dyer to endorse my book," I said. "Then I'll be all set!"

He was quiet for a moment. Then he asked, "Do you want to meet him?"

"Of course I want to meet him," I replied. "But I'm pretty sure he lives on Maui."

"You can meet him next week," he told me. "My wife, Amanda, grew up next door to his family in Boca Raton. She is a close friend of his daughter, Serena. We're going to a charity dinner, and Wayne will be there. You should come."

The only answer I could muster was an ecstatic scream.

The next week, I was at a dinner with Dr. Wayne Dyer, the father of manifestation. My number one mentor was in the room with me!

Will and Grace were both with me as I was introduced to him, and we instantly fell into a wonderful conversation. He spoke about

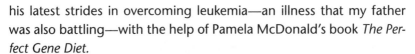

his latest strides in overcoming leukemia—an illness that my father was also battling—with the help of Pamela McDonald's book *The Perfect Gene Diet.*

When I went to say good-bye to Dr. Dyer that evening, I told him that I'd written a book about manifestation. I asked if he would consider reading it and offering his advice.

His eyes lit up. "It would be a pleasure," he said. "Ask Serena for my home address, and send the book to me."

I walked into the bathroom. Will waited outside (it was a ladies' room, after all), but Grace came in with me. She looked at me and said, *Jennifer! Well done!*

Will helped you write the book, Grace said. *And I was glad to bring you this moment. How do you feel?*

I broke down and cried. I was overwhelmed with gratitude for Grace's work in orchestrating this divine appointment.

The events following that day were also full of Will and Grace. Dr. Dyer quickly responded to my manuscript. He hated my title at the time, which was *1, 2, 3 Manifest!* He suggested that I focus the title around the acting techniques I use to help tap into the emotional state of manifesting goals. The next morning, Grace whispered in my ear: *Jen, the new title of your book will be <u>Directing Your Destiny: How to Become the Writer, Producer, and Director of Your Dreams.</u>*

I called Serena and asked her to pass my thanks along to her dad. During our call, she suggested that I attend a Hay House Writer's Workshop in San Diego. One person from the workshop would be awarded a publishing contract, and Serena thought I'd be a good contender. I thanked her profusely and registered for the workshop.

The experience was amazing. I learned the nitty-gritty of the publishing world from Hay House president Reid Tracy and *New York Times* best-selling author Cheryl Richardson.

I also left knowing that Will and I had our work cut out for us.

The next morning at 5:30, the event on my phone calendar asked, "Jen, do you really want it?"

I had three months to write a book proposal. As it turned out, writing the proposal was even harder than writing my book! But luckily, I had my dream team on hand to help. As my good friend and colleague Erika Miscio always says, "It takes a village to build an empire!"

The day finally arrived when Hay House would announce the contest winner. I felt confident. I just knew that I'd put together a winning package. I checked the Hay House Facebook page every hour. I checked my phone every half hour between that. Finally, at 7:00 P.M., a winner was announced.

It was not me.

Faith Freed, author of *IS: Your Authentic Spirituality Unleashed,* was the winner. I logged on to her website. Faith was cool, authentic, and smart. At least I had lost to a really amazing woman.

Still, I cried.

Grace came and sat next to me. *It's her time,* she said. *Yours will come. Let go of attachment. Surrender to this moment. Accept it for what it is.*

I allowed myself to be sad for 24 hours. Then, two weeks later, Will and I got on a plane to New York City. We were going to attend the Hay House Movers and Shakers workshop. It was another opportunity to win a publishing contract.

Will and I refused to be defeated. We were going to pick ourselves up, brush ourselves off, and submit our proposal all over again.

For the next two months, Will and I worked with my team to rewrite my proposal. I got a national television spot on a talk show. We also built my social-media empire, with more than 5,000 people following my every move.

We were not going to give up.

On December 20, 2011—almost one year to the day after my mountaintop manifestation session in Sedona—Reid Tracy called.

"Welcome to the Hay House family," he said. "You won!"

It was one of the happiest days of my life. Will, Grace, and the rest of my dream team celebrated with a bottle of champagne.

I learned that getting a book published is almost as difficult as winning the lottery. But when you're engaged with action and surrender, Will and Grace will get you there.

The Universal Law of Action

Will and Grace are not magic, but their effect is certainly magical. By learning when to call in Will and knowing when to stand with

Grace, you can use both to become the director of your destiny. You just need to invite them in. I promise they will come.

During Week IV, we will explore the three practices of the Universal Law of Action: cultivating will, cultivating grace, and cultivating gratitude. This law is frequently overlooked. If there is no action behind our dreams, they are simply daydreams. When action is applied, they become manifested reality.

The practices from Weeks I through III are a necessary foundation for finding your true dreams. They also allow you to communicate those dreams to Source. That is how you create the best movie of your life. Week IV will teach you how to put these realized dreams into action.

Practice 7

GETTING OFF THE COUCH: CULTIVATING THE WILL TO REALIZE YOUR DREAMS

"What you can do, or dream you can, begin it;
Boldness has genius, power, and magic in it."

— JOHANN VON GOETHE

When I was sitting on the couch trying to manifest my perfect life through a vision board, I didn't yet realize I had to get off that couch to assist Source in collaborating with me. This collaboration is what I now call "The Art of Getting off the Couch."

I am now quite proficient at this particular art. Many of my friends have marveled at my ability to make things happen. They think I possess some magical ability.

I don't. I simply leap . . . then look . . . and then figure it all out.

You must get off the couch in order for your dreams and visions to be realized. Bringing in Will produces tangible results. He is a necessary component to manifesting your dreams. If you only read your intentions, play your mind movie, and meditate, nothing will happen.

If I had just visualized being a Hay House author, for example, it would not have happened.

I had to get off the couch—or, in that case, out of bed—and actually write the book, go to California and New York, and write not one but two book proposals.

Overcoming the Fear of Getting off the Couch

Many of us have crystal clear dreams. We are just too afraid to get off the couch and live them out. Our fears are usually disguised as excuses about why we cannot live our dreams at any particular moment. My excuse was that I didn't have time to write a book. Another common one is that we're waiting for something to happen before we go after our dreams. We wait because things are not yet "perfect" or because we're not sure "how to go about it" yet. Too often, we wait because our dreams seem too risky.

Every excuse for waiting is brought to you by the Itty-Bitty Shitty Committee.

When I launched my retreat company, most people thought I was crazy. I just picked a destination, made a flyer, got on a plane, and took 18 people to Sedona. I had no website. I had no experience running a retreat. All I had was a business partner who could teach yoga and my own transformational-workshop skills. I prepared as best I could for the retreat. I knew, however, that my experience would teach me how to lead it.

If we had waited for everything to be perfect, we might have waited forever. Instead, we launched the retreat company just two months after the initial idea was born.

Yes, I was terrified that it would be a failure. But I didn't allow that fear to paralyze me. Instead, I felt the fear and did it anyway. If it didn't go well, I thought, it would still be a powerful learning experience. Well, it turned out to be a smashing success: our participants left feeling relaxed, transformed, and recharged. Since that retreat, we've taken it all over the world: Greece, Italy, Bali, Costa Rica, and Cambodia!

We always have a choice: Go for something or allow our excuses to stop us.

Here are five ways to overcome your fear of getting off the couch!

1. Stop Making Excuses

Anything worthwhile will have an element of risk. The more we cultivate intuition during meditation, however, the better we become at silencing our Committee. Then we can clearly hear what the best next steps will be.

Risk is minimized when you listen to intuition. Your intuitive voice will always steer you in the right direction. You just need to differentiate between the voices of your Committee and your voice of intuition. Both are inside your head. The more you do the work outlined here, the better you will be at determining whether your Committee or your intuition is speaking up.

Here's a real-life example: My client Emily is a naturopath who wanted to host her own Internet-radio show, but she kept holding herself back, saying, "I would do it, but I don't know how."

I told her to mute her Committee and advised, "Go online and find five other radio-show hosts. E-mail them, and ask them ten questions about how to host and market an online show. Then, hold a mock radio show and invite your family and friends."

In short, I took away her excuse.

Too many risks and too little money are also frequent excuses for refusing to get off the couch. The only money I spent when I first launched my business was for printing. And even that was at cost, thanks to a good friend who introduced me to a great printer. Instead, I bartered in the beginning. I gave my dream team free coaching and courses, and in turn they helped me build my website, market my classes, and edit my brochures. People are always interested in helping. Be creative. You may have something they want, too. You'll never know until you ask.

2. Ask for Help

Many people are just afraid to ask for help. For them, I have two things to say:

The worst thing that could happen is that someone says no. And the best thing that could happen is that asking for help puts you on the path to success.

When I began coaching, I asked ten established coaches if I could buy them coffee and learn how they began their careers. Everyone said yes. They willingly gave their time, and many of those 20-minute coffee meetings turned into hour-long advice sessions.

People love to share the secrets to their success and the pitfalls they experienced along the way. Those who relied on shared wisdom from their own mentors are, in turn, happy to mentor new people, too.

If you reach a point of uncertainty, ask an expert. Find someone who has done what you'd like to do, and ask that person for help.

3. Call in Support

You must identify the obstacles that are preventing you from taking action. Call in support, and ask someone to hold you accountable for follow-through. You'll quickly learn that these obstacles are the creation of your Itty-Bitty Shitty Committee. Just as you're about to ask a potential mentor out for coffee, the Committee says, *Don't call this person; he (or she) doesn't want to be bothered.*

To overcome the Committee, be prepared and ready for the list of excuses it will throw at you. Call in support, and surround yourself with friends or family who will hold you accountable. When you keep quiet and hide your dreams, those who love you and want you to succeed will never know if you've realized your goals or not. When you tell everyone what you're up to, though, they'll help you follow through.

Set a date for your goals, and share those dates with someone close to you, asking him or her to check in with you just before the date arrives. It will help you get things done.

A life coach is also a great person to hold you accountable. If you cannot afford a coach, ask a friend who is also working on his or her goals to fill in. Schedule a Monday morning accountability call, in which you report to each other on the steps you've taken. You can also brainstorm how to make progress together and devise strategies for the upcoming week. Cheer each other on through the process, and support each other during the struggles.

You can accomplish your dreams on your own, but when you join forces with others, you'll reach them even faster.

4. Do Something Outrageous

When we do something outside of our comfort zone, it flows into all the other areas of our lives as well. For instance, once I had walked on hot coals and been certified in scuba diving, asking a well-known published author to tell me his or her secret to success didn't seem so intimidating.

I have devised a list of 30 things you can do. There are 10 slightly outrageous things, 10 pretty outrageous things, and 10 *completely* outrageous things.

This week, choose one from the slightly outrageous list. Then, select something from one of the lists each month for the next year. Consider doing five or six slightly outrageous things over the first five or six months, five or six pretty outrageous things the next five or six months, and then at least one thing from the completely outrageous list by the end of the year. You can even enroll your friends and family to join you. Have fun with them, and remember, you are a spiritual warrior.

Here are ten slightly outrageous things to do:

1. Plant a tree and dedicate it to someone you love.
2. Go out to a fancy dinner by yourself.
3. Build a giant sand castle at the beach.
4. Visit a fortune-teller.
5. Get up early and watch the sunrise.
6. Sleep outside under the stars.
7. Go salsa dancing.
8. Take a tango lesson.
9. Send a message in a bottle.
10. Make an anonymous donation.

Here are ten pretty outrageous things to do:

1. Spend the entire day in silence.

2. Ride a motorcycle.

3. Learn to play an instrument.

4. Go skinny-dipping.

5. Book a trip to a historic site, such as Stonehenge or the Coliseum, or to see the Northern Lights in Alaska.

6. Climb a mountain.

7. Learn a foreign language.

8. Forgive someone you never thought you'd forgive.

9. Fast for the day.

10. Dance in the pouring rain.

Here are ten completely outrageous things to do:

1. Jump off a cliff into the ocean.

2. Get certified in scuba diving.

3. Go on a safari.

4. Go skydiving.

5. Go shark-cage diving.

6. Ride in a hot-air balloon.

7. Go white-water rafting.

8. Ride a camel in the desert.

9. Make love with your partner on an airplane. (Note that you may get in big trouble for this, though, so be sure you can get away with it!)

10. Walk a tightrope.

It's not important what you do. It's just important that you do it. When you begin to engage in outrageous activities, the rest of life seems less frightening.

5. Change Your Language

Becoming the director of your dreams means having the ability to make empowering choices. Just as a film director must know which decision will make the film a masterpiece, you must also learn to exercise that same skill. When you do, new paths will be revealed. As you walk some of those paths, however, you may find a few crossroads.

If you're exploring a new career path, you may discover that you're uncertain about the training necessary for that job. Or, if you realize you'd like to move, you may not immediately know the best destination for you.

These crossroads can seem intimidating, because we look at them as decisions to be made, which often makes us feel as if we're in a pressure cooker. We become paralyzed about making a "wrong" decision.

Think about this: life isn't made up of decisions; it's made up of experiences.

Instead of saying, "I have a decision to make," try saying, "I have a choice to make." The very definition of *decision* is the act or need for making up one's mind. *Choice* is defined as the power, right, or liberty to choose.

You evoke a different energy when you say you need to make up your mind. Instead, think about saying that you have the liberty to choose. Liberty means freedom. Similarly, decisions hold the weight of finality, while choices feel more open and relaxed.

If you choose an experience and it turns out to not be the best choice, you can always choose again. As you replace the word *decision* with *choice,* you will feel less pressure about the crossroads before you.

It's not always easy forging ahead toward the life of your dreams. Using these five tools, one step at a time, will make the journey easier.

EEE

We must learn to transform the stagnant areas of our lives so they can begin to flow. This requires taking action to shift what no longer works for us.

A great tool that I teach in the Creative Insight Journey for identifying areas in which we may be stuck is the EEE test. It works for
evaluating careers, friendships, relationships, and homes.

The three E's are *Ease, Energy,* and *Enjoyment.*

The first E, *Ease,* should not be confused with *easy.* Sitting on the
couch is easy, but it will not manifest your dreams. Ease is about working toward your intentions by doing what you love. You should feel at
ease when you are around your friends and in your home.

Romantic relationships, for example, are not *easy* to sustain, but
there should be an ease to them. Writing this book was not easy. It
meant beginning work at 5:30 each morning. When I did so, however, the writing gracefully flowed out of me with ease.

Think about how you feel at work, at home, or with your friends
or partner. Is there an ease, or do these things feel challenging? Put
them to the test.

The next E, *Energy,* can be measured by asking whether something feels heavy or light. From friendships to relationships, it's
important to ensure that our personal connections aren't weighing
us down. We can measure the energy of any situation by asking ourselves, *Does this make me feel heavy or light?* It's a quick way to intuit
whether something is right or wrong for you.

A great way to transform heavy energy at home is to move furniture, clear clutter, and brighten the walls with a new paint job. We can
also lighten the energy of our relationships by clearing things up with
an honest conversation. We can even transform heavy energy at the
office with fresh creativity, humor, or meditation breaks.

The last E, *Enjoyment,* is about being happy with your relationships, home, and work. Is your journey leading you to the life of your
dreams? If it is, even the most difficult work will be enjoyable.

If you find that a particular area of your life—be it a relationship,
your home, or your job—remains heavy even after repeated attempts
at transformation, it may be time to reevaluate. This can be a sign that
it's time to move, find a new job, or leave a relationship. In that case,
use the fourth *E: Exit!*

EEE will become a compass for your life. Put your relationships,
home, and work to the EEE test. If anything doesn't measure up to all
three, find a way to transform it. If that doesn't work, let it go.

Put some sticky notes up during Week IV to remind you of the EEE test. Also, try putting a reminder on a mirror, a computer, or on a car visor. It's a great way to check in and ensure that your life is in alignment with all three E's.

DreamStorming and How, What, and When

For each intention you set, you must have action steps to bring it to fruition. The DreamStorming and How, What, and When tools will help you get off the couch. If you have an especially big intention, it can sometimes feel overwhelming. By using these tools, though, you'll learn to break down your action steps in a way that makes everything more doable.

The story of my student Laura is a perfect example of this process:

Her intention was to become a professional stylist. When Laura first set this intention, she was working a nine-to-five job as an administrative assistant. She knew her passion was for styling, because she got great joy from helping friends select outfits, organize closets, and shop for the perfect accessories. Laura had a knack for styling and was confident that she could turn this skill into a profitable profession.

I advised her to keep her day job while we launched her new business, which was to work as a stylist on the weekends. There were many action steps necessary to realize her new career, and we began our work with a *DreamStorm*—which is what I call a brainstorming session related to a particular dream.

We took the steps identified during the DreamStorm and turned them into an action plan. That plan identified the How, What, and When action steps Laura would need to take. Within six months, Laura was able to leave her day job and become a successful full-time stylist.

Now, do your own DreamStorm.

Take a blank sheet of paper and write an intention in the middle. Then, fill the rest of the space with the action steps you'll need to take in order to make your dream a reality.

In Laura's case, she began with "successful personal stylist" as her intention. The rest of her DreamStorm sheet included steps related to opening a bank account, registering a website, creating a logo, and building a budget and business plan. Your DreamStorm exercise should include three action steps that are high priority as you begin working toward your goals.

Here is Laura's DreamStorm:

After you've completed your DreamStorm and identified your first three action steps, you will need to use the How, What, and When tool. This is a step-by-step process for accomplishing your dreams, and it will help you track your progress by recording the date and time you complete each step.

In Laura's case, the *What* was creating a budget; the *How* was a spreadsheet to track expenses for her new business; and the *When* was the deadline for completing the spreadsheet, which she identified as September 1.

Every intention needs a good, strong plan to be fully realized. It requires clear thinking, a strong belief system, and alignment of your own state of mind and what you want to attract. We must be in action every step of the way. Here are three common how, what, and when action steps:

Action 1

What: I feel at peace that I am now financially responsible.

How: I will create a budget for myself so that I will not overspend.

When: By May 1, 2012

Action 2

What: I feel at peace that I am now financially responsible.

How: I will get a second job that pays $2,000 per month.

When: By June 15, 2012

Action 3

What: I feel at peace that I am now financially responsible.

How: I will pay off one credit card at a time with that extra $2,000 each month.

When: By May 1, 2013, I will be debt free!

These were my first three How, What, and When plans as I began writing this book:

Action 1

What: I feel ecstatic that I am now a published Hay House author.

How: I will wake up at 5:30 A.M. each day and write for one hour.

When: I will complete my first draft by June 1, 2011.

Action 2

What: I feel ecstatic that I am now a published Hay House author.

How: I will wake up daily at 5:30 A.M. and dedicate one hour to writing my book proposal.

When: I will submit my proposal by October 15, 2012.

Action 3

What: I feel ecstatic that I am now a published Hay House author.

How: I will wake up every day at 5:30 A.M. and write 555 words.

When: I will submit my 50,000-word, polished manuscript by January 15, 2013.

Having a plan like this creates the accountability and clarity needed in order to bring your intentions to fruition.

You can even create a How, What, and When plan to clarify exactly what you want. If you are hoping to change careers, for example, but do not yet know your life's purpose, your action plan might look like this:

Action 1

What: I feel thrilled that I am now crystal clear about my life's purpose.

How: I will talk to five people who are already in my new field to learn about their careers.

When: I will contact five people by April 3 and complete my conversations with them by April 20.

Action 2

What: I feel thrilled that I am now crystal clear about my life's purpose.

How: I will meditate for 30 consecutive days to open myself to more clarity and insight.

When: I will meditate each day until May 30.

Action 3

What: I feel thrilled that I am now crystal clear about my life's purpose.

How: I will hire a life coach to help me discover what my purpose might be.

When: I will have my first life-coaching session by April 15.

Now it's your turn!

Your six intention cards show *what* you're intending. Now you need to discover the *how* and *when*. The first six practices in this book are the groundwork for communicating to Source what you want. In order for it to deliver that to you, however, you'll need to do your part.

Remember that the movie you're creating is a collaboration with Source. Your job is to take action by taking responsibility and getting off the couch. When you do, momentum begins to shift in your favor.

"But I don't know what to do first," my students sometimes protest.

"It doesn't matter what you do first," I remind them. "Just do *something!*"

Take a moment to write three How, What, and When plans for each of your six intentions. Then work these steps into your daily schedule. Each week, take the necessary steps to cross one action off your list.

Turning your intention into reality may involve 50—or even more!—action steps. Do not be overwhelmed. Just follow this step-by-step process:

1. Write them all down.

2. Prioritize them.

3. Create How, What, and When plans for the three steps that are most immediately important.

When you have completed these steps, write three more. Break them into pieces, take small bites, and stay on track.

Director's Notes

❋ Stop waiting. Just take action. Silencing your Committee will move you toward becoming the director of your life.

❋ Use EEE as a compass. It will help keep you in alignment with what makes you truly happy and fulfilled.

❋ Don't be afraid to ask for help. Train yourself by doing small acts that take you outside of your comfort zone.

❋ How, What, and When is a powerful tool for breaking down your action steps and creating the best movie of your life.

NONATTACHMENT: CULTIVATING GRACE AND SURRENDERING YOUR DREAMS

*"Our realization only happens in the present moment.
To be here fully, we must be willing to let go of the past and
meet the future with open arms. That often means letting
the doors that brought us here close behind us."*

— PAUL FERRINI

Enlightenment brings complete happiness and contentment. You no longer have attachments to anyone or anything.

As I age, my own attachments to people and things have lessened; however, I'm nowhere near fully enlightened. When I was married, happiness for me was a four-and-a-half-carat diamond ring, Prada shoes, and a Mercedes-Benz. After my divorce, happiness was redefined as time with my son, dinner with friends, and savoring a good book while relaxing in my hammock.

All of these things, of course, can be taken away in one fell swoop. Friends and family may move away or die, hammocks get ripped apart in hurricanes, and the lease on a Mercedes must inevitably come to an end. So when I define happiness today, I focus on things that cannot be taken away. Creativity, humor, and quiet stillness are very much a part of what brings me joy. These are the things no storm, death, or finance company can take away.

This is what the Buddhists call "unshakable happiness." It is about a state of being in which you are, first and foremost, happy with yourself. Everything comes from within.

Of course, I do still find happiness in the material world and my personal relationships. But I no longer look to them as the source of my happiness. The more I can be content with myself, the more I can look to outside forces as a cherry on top of my cake, rather than the cake itself.

When I was manifesting my current love relationship, I made a list of the qualities I wanted in a partner. They included charisma, confidence, kindness, ambition, power, humor, adventure, and open-mindedness, among others. When I looked at the list, I realized that I already possess each of those qualities. I didn't need to manifest a man to bring me happiness, because I already had what I was looking for within. He might have been the cherry on the cake, but I was the cake itself.

The Practice of Nonattachment

Before we define *nonattachment,* we must learn to recognize its opposite.

Attachment is when we hold on to things, feeling as if we cannot live without them. We believe that our happiness depends on them.

What are you overly attached to? Are they physical things, like cars, houses, or even people? Or are they mental attachments to things such as your name, career, or belief system? You may even be spiritually attached, such as to a religion or a guru.

It's necessary to identify our attachments in order to realize what we're holding on to or trying to find happiness in. Many times, we experience pain and suffering when we lose things that we're attached to. By practicing nonattachment, we can avoid some of that pain and suffering by refusing to be attached to their source.

Nonattachment is the powerful Buddhist concept of no longer seeking things for pleasure or avoiding things that cause pain. When we're detached from life, we go with the flow. We still enjoy things, but we enjoy them as they come.

When a particular moment in the movie of your life brings great pleasure, enjoy it. But enjoy it in the present moment. Do not try and hold on to the pleasure. Simply appreciate it as it is. Do not wonder if, or when, it will return. The same goes for pain. If you experience a painful moment in your movie, move through it. When it passes, do not worry if it will ever come back again.

Nonattachment can be a difficult practice to undertake. Most of us, myself included, are control freaks. We demand to know how and when things will happen. We want to know how everything will work out. Most important, we desperately hold on to the things we think bring us joy.

Now, please realize that there's nothing wrong with that. But we must be aware that everything changes. Nothing stays the same. Life's only certainty is uncertainty. When we embody this philosophy, we no longer feel insulted or hurt when things do change. We understand that nothing lasts forever. It's then that we can be grateful for joys that we experience, because we know that any joy may eventually pass.

The practice of nonattachment must be applied to your six intentions, too. It's critical that you drop any expectations about how your intentions, or future-life scripts, are going to play out. You must surrender.

Yes, I know I've told you to set intentions, write future-life scripts, and create action steps. And yes, I am also telling you to simultaneously let go of any expectation about how those things will all come to fruition.

It may seem counterintuitive, but that's what must be done.

After all the work and preparation has been done, we must detach ourselves from the final outcome. Our energy is out of alignment when we're too attached. We become fixated and desperate. We think that we've failed if our expectations are not met exactly as we intended. This is when we must trust that Source is always conspiring with us and knows better than we do.

I currently intend to be a *New York Times* best-selling author. But underneath that lofty goal is my *real* intention: to make a difference in the lives of millions by sharing knowledge and information about manifestation.

I also realize, however, that Source knows better than I do. It knows which path is the surest for me. I trust it to put me in situations where I can motivate, inspire, and share knowledge with seekers around the world. Source may lead me to a television show, a radio program, or some other format that allows me to impact the lives of others. Throughout the process of manifesting my intention, I must remain detached from any specific outcome, including seeing my name on the *New York Times* best-seller list.

In every situation, there are millions of possibilities. I must trust—and keep trusting—that Source will reveal the best one for me.

Trusting Source

Our thoughts and wishes must be clearly expressed if we want Source to collaborate with us in making our intentions a reality. Then, once that hard work is done, we must let go of any expectations about how those intentions will be delivered. Flexibility, and even blind trust, is required if we want to receive all the gifts available to us.

If we're seeking love and expecting it to come in the form of a tall, dark, and handsome stranger, we'll be disappointed when a short, chubby, and hilarious version shows up. But, if we stay with just the *intention* of love, we won't miss it when it arrives. We must remain in wonder and be open to whatever gift Source has sent our way.

When you encounter disappointment or obstacles in your manifestation work, trust that everything is in divine order, rather than question why it's not going your way. Have you ever found yourself in a horrible situation, such as ending a relationship or being fired from a job, and thought you had the worst luck in the world? Later, you probably discovered that this "bad luck" led to a dream job or a magical new relationship. If we stay in our old energy, new possibilities will never arrive.

Source knows better than we do.

When things don't go my way, I choose to trust that things will come around in the end. That's surrender. It's about being open to new possibilities when current ones aren't working out. Surrendering means allowing things to unfold organically and gracefully.

Take a moment now to review your six intention cards. Study your intentions, one by one, and identify any feelings of desperation regarding their outcomes. Ask if you can still be happy if they do not come to fruition. If the answer is no, then there's work to be done. Start each day by saying to yourself, *I already have all the happiness I need deep inside me. Anything that comes to me is simply the cherry on the cake.*

My intention to become a Hay House author wasn't attached to a specific outcome. If Hay House had rejected my book, I would have been disappointed. But one door's closing would have forced me to open another. I had to fully trust that Source was divinely guiding me to where I should be, that every no is secretly guiding me to a perfect yes.

We also cannot take a no personally. In the big picture, everything is perfect as it is. We must surrender to Source and trust that it's looking out for our best interests. We may not know why things are happening as they are, but we usually look back and say, "Thank goodness that happened, because now I'm doing what I love."

My student Brian found himself in a very sticky situation until he finally learned to trust Source. An aspiring rap artist told Brian, who was working in real estate, that he had a surefire hit record. Brian listened to the rapper's remake of the Journey hit "Don't Stop Believin'" and thought it would be a big hit, too. He set out to raise half a million dollars for an album, tour, and marketing campaign. Brian put his full trust in the project and asked 26 of his family, friends, and business associates to help.

Then, Brian found out that he'd been conned.

Unbeknownst to him, obtaining the rights to a hit song can be very, very expensive. Most record labels, he was told, would most likely not pay for an unknown artist to obtain those rights to use that music with new lyrics sung over them. Before he could tell his rapper that he wanted to pull the plug on the deal, all of the money was gone.

The people who had loaned Brian the funds for his project began asking when those loans would be repaid. One associate threatened a lawsuit. Every day, the phone rang with the same threat. Brian spent hours on each call, begging for more time to repay.

When Brian first told me about what was happening, I thought it sounded a lot like blackmail. The investor had been threatening to sue for over six months, but had never done so. Instead, he was vying for Brian's attention, keeping him on the phone for hours each day. But it didn't seem that the stress and anxiety Brian was experiencing was worth it.

"Call the guy's bluff," I said. "Let the cards fall where they may."

Brian followed my advice. He told the investor he would no longer be taking his calls. He went back to his work as a high-end real-estate agent. The lawsuit was never filed. The man realized that Brian was also a victim of the situation.

Within two months, Brian had sold more real estate than in the entire previous year. He finally had the money to pay back half the funds to each of his 26 investors. Because he had let go and stopped fearing the situation, Source provided the money he needed to make things right.

Today, Brian has a thriving and successful real-estate business. He is also confident that, by the end of the year, all his investors will be paid in full.

When we trust Source and let go of our attachment to the things and people no longer serving us, we can live in peace. When we live in peace, we can be open to the ever-present abundance in our lives.

Letting Go

We often hear directors shouting, "Cut!" This sometimes happens when the director has filmed a performance that's not right for the film. Then, with another take, or several, the director gets the desired performance.

What do you need to cut from your life? Do you have a particularly negative friend who depletes your energy? Are you in a relationship that lacks joy, love, or respect? Or are you holding on to disappointing situations that you haven't been able to get over?

These attachments may be blocking new energy from coming in. If you let go of disappointment, it will be immediately replaced by something more positive. You'll get the take that you want.

It's imperative to trust in Source and not hold on to the old out of fear. Everything has a cycle. Just as we are born, grow old, and die, every aspect of our lives follows a similar path. When we hold on to things that are dying, we only prolong a heavy death.

Ceremonies can be a helpful way to detach from something. Here are a few that I often use:

Dig a Hole

Find a photo or something that symbolizes what you need to detach from. Then dig a small hole and place the object into it. As you cover it with dirt, think about how grateful you are for the lessons it has taught you. Then reflect on why it no longer serves you.

When the object is buried, place a flower or crystal over it, say good-bye, and walk away. Never look back.

Write the Story

Writing is also another powerful way to let go. Write the story of how a relationship, situation, or event has played out. Fill it with your hurt, anger, and fear. Start with the journal prompt "What happened was . . ." and pour your emotions into it.

Then read it aloud to yourself or a friend. Do this repeatedly until you feel no emotional charge during your reading. Become immune to its meaning. Make it meaningless. Then, light the paper on fire and release it into the wind.

Visit the Ocean

Water has very healing properties and can powerfully assist in the letting-go process. Next time you are near a lake or ocean, lie in the sand with your legs stretched out into the water. As the water rushes in, think about what you want to let go of, and when the water rushes back out, imagine it carrying away what no longer serves you. Do this over and over until you feel complete.

Identify one thing this week that's no longer serving you. Choose one of the rituals just described to let it go. Then, watch Source respond and deliver new and exciting adventures in your life.

Remember to honor the feelings you experience when you let go. Ask those who love you to support you through the process.

This isn't about leaving a job, ending a friendship, or filing for divorce. It's about letting go of the emotions linked to those situations and relationships. Once you've done that, ask Source to help remove you from these situations when the time is right. Since manifestation is about seeing, believing, and then feeling, we can start by taking small but necessary actions on the journey to realizing our new reality.

Nonattachment is a lifelong pursuit. It can be a slow process to let go of something you believe has brought you great happiness. Throughout, be clear about who you are and what you want. In the last moments, surrender and trust Source. The final details will be those that benefit you the most.

Source will help you transform, evolve, and grow.

Nonattachment as a Daily Practice

Each week, we have built upon our meditation and manifestation routines by incorporating seven different practices into that work. The eighth practice is nonattachment. This practice is about a way of being, rather than a state of doing.

Work this practice into your daily routine by always checking in with yourself. Do it while reading your intention cards. Make sure your happiness is not dependent upon a specific path to fruition.

Instead, return to a state of gratitude. When we're consistently grateful for life as it is, Source delivers what's best for us. When an intention becomes reality, as I said earlier, it's the cherry on the cake rather than the cake itself.

Take some time to identify what you need to let go of, and do the burying, writing, or water ritual to assist you in finding closure with this particular issue.

Director's Notes

⁕ Begin cultivating true happiness by finding resources of happiness within yourself. When we look for happiness through material things or relationships, we can fall into traps.

⁕ Use the practice of nonattachment to turn your intentions of peace, joy, love, and abundance into reality. Allow Source to divinely orchestrate how this will happen. Let go of expectations about how things will turn out. Be open to the delightful surprises that Source has in store for you.

⁕ Let go of what no longer serves you, and clear the way for your intentions to manifest.

⁕ Rituals help you to let go and begin the process of surrender and release.

Practice 9

UNLIMITED ABUNDANT FLOW: CULTIVATING GRATITUDE TO APPRECIATE YOUR DREAMS

"You have no cause for anything but gratitude and joy."

— BUDDHA

When you fully embrace gratitude, the most amazing moments of your life arrive. The birth of my son, my being invited into the Screen Actors Guild, and my being welcomed to the Hay House family were all times of great gratitude.

Those days, of course, are easy to accept with gratitude. The real work lies in living in a state of gratitude *every day*, and especially when we don't feel like it.

If we're focused on how much we have, rather than what we don't have, we slide into the flow of universal abundance. We exit that flow in times of obsession about our needs and wants. Instead, we must train ourselves to constantly be in awe of, and have appreciation for, what's right in front of us.

There are times when gratitude seems impossible. It's hard to be grateful when we lose a home, a loved one, or a job. Yet, if we continue to focus on what we lack, we only attract more lack.

Many people become confused when working with the Universal Laws of Attention, Attraction, and Action. They are so focused on what they want to manifest in the future that they forget to be grateful for the present.

It's important not to fall into that trap. If you're in a constant state of wanting what you don't have, Source will simply give you more things to want. Instead, if you want happiness, be happy. If you need peace, be peaceful. The more you live in the emotional state of what you want, the easier it will flow to you.

When I feel particularly down, I remind myself to stop the "poor me" act. For a few moments, I force myself to be grateful that I have a warm bed, food to eat, and eyes with which to see. Most of us take these things for granted, even though there are plenty of people in the world who do not have these luxuries.

I try, every day, to feel as if I have won the lottery. I was born in a country where I have modern conveniences, freedom, and opportunity. Those are essential things to be grateful for.

I also volunteer with Women in Distress, working with women who have been abused and are homeless. My work there makes me aware of just how much I do have. I am grateful that I can help them. I feel so fortunate later, when I am safe and warm in my bed. My worries and problems seem insignificant and small in comparison.

I also say thank you for a new day each morning when I get out of bed. Then, before I go to sleep in the evening, I list five things from the day that I'm grateful to have experienced. By ending my day in gratitude, I am far less likely to toss and turn throughout the night. Instead, I fall asleep with gratitude in my heart. That, in turn, seeps into my dreams. I wake up with zest and enthusiasm for a new day.

Gratitude Practice

It is important to reflect once each day on the things for which you are grateful. Incorporate this into your meditation and manifestation routine. Each night, reflect on your gratitude in your journal.

Find five things that you can be grateful for that you have or have experienced. Write your list, and then read it again. Let genuine appreciation wash over you. Feel gratitude, and stay with that feeling.

Here are five things I was grateful for last night after returning from a party with friends:

- ※ I am grateful for the beautiful cheese plate I shared with my friends.
- ※ I am grateful for our laughter while playing the game Catch Phrase.
- ※ I am grateful for my beautiful relationship with my son.
- ※ I am grateful that my mammogram results came back okay.
- ※ I am grateful for all the love I receive from my family and friends.

Do this gratitude practice every night in your journal right before you go to sleep.

Turning Frustration into Gratitude

Life is filled with events that can lead you out of a state of peace, love, and gratitude. If you catch yourself in one of these situations, it's quite easy to bring yourself back.

If you're waiting in a line that's not moving, choose not to be aggravated or frustrated. Instead, turn to the person next to you and be grateful for having someone in your life. If you're on hold, waiting an hour or more for a customer-service agent, don't pull your hair out. Instead, pause to appreciate a work of art that's in your line of vision or even to be grateful for the roof over your head.

Even when you find yourself in an argument with a particularly difficult person, see it as an opportunity to practice patience, tolerance, and forgiveness.

There is always something you can be grateful for, even in the most irritating moments. Remind yourself to do this practice by tying a blue string (symbolizing peace and gratitude) around your wrist.

It can become your touchstone for remembering that there's always something to be grateful for.

Generosity

Have you ever noticed that it's those who give abundantly who also live in abundance? Generosity does that. If we don't give of our time or money, the flow stops. Even if it stems from a fear of not having enough, it will cut off our connection with universal abundance.

One of the first things I ask my students to do is clean out their closets and give away anything they no longer need. I also ask them to give away something very dear to their hearts.

When they release material things, they report feeling clearer, lighter, and happier. When they choose to give away something dear to them, they're warmed by the grateful smile on the recipient's face.

Every day I try to give something to someone. It may be as small as a smile, or an act of kindness as simple as holding a door or paying for someone's meal. I've even paid the parking meter for someone I've never met.

Small acts can make our hearts sing. When that happens, we're filled with the joy of giving. We fall into a state of love and gratitude. In turn, Source sends love and gratitude back to us in many different forms.

Never give to receive, though. You'll be happily surprised when you give with only the intention of giving.

The Practice of Giving

Give something to someone every day, even beyond the four weeks of this course. Whether it's simple or significant, give with no expectation of getting anything back. In fact, by the end of Week IV, see if you can find something that you possess that's very meaningful to you, and give it away.

Here are some selfless acts of giving to get you started:

* Clean out your closet. Give away everything you haven't used in the past year.

* Give away something that has sentimental value to you.

✳ Call five people you love and tell them you love them.

✳ Find a local charity and volunteer your time.

✳ Give a percentage of your income to charity.

✳ Give an anonymous gift.

When we are aware of the value of small things, we realize what's truly important.

Let's end with a meditation to open your heart. This is a meditation you can do anytime you feel that you're closing your heart down. You may want to have someone read it to you, or you may record it yourself. You can also download a free MP3 version on my website **www.thecenterofgrace.com/meditation**.

Love and Gratitude Meditation

Find a quiet place where you can lie down. Start taking long, deep breaths. You have nowhere to go and nowhere to be except right here, right now.

Imagine that you are lying in a beautiful field. You can see the tall grass around you. A blanket of peace washes over your entire body as you sink deep into the earth.

You don't have a care in the world. All is well.

You settle in with your hands behind your head, and you begin to watch the clouds passing. A smile spreads across your face. All your intentions have come to fruition. As you think back on all that has occurred and all that you have created, you realize that the doing has been done.

You have experienced your wildest dreams and your greatest aspirations. Immense peace surrounds your entire being. You feel your body giving itself to the earth. You feel yourself relaxing in surrender. Then you feel grateful to have had the opportunity to realize these dreams. You are grateful that you had the support, love, and resources when you needed them the most.

Place your attention on your heart. Imagine your heart enclosed by a flower. Then, with each inhalation and each exhalation, allow one petal to open at a time. As the petal opens on each out breath, feel your body sinking deeper into the earth. Allow the flower to open, revealing a beautiful pink light. As this pink light begins to spill out and around your body, you feel an enormous amount of love wash over your entire being.

Imagine this light spreading out over the field and touching all the people you love. Then, bring all of the love in your heart even farther out, and touch all of the people you are acquainted with, such as your co-workers and neighbors. Send all the love in your heart out to them.

With each breath, your love expands. Extend this blanket of love over the entire city you live in. Create an energetic frequency of love all around you. Allow this love to spread over the entire country, sending it out to people who may need more love in their lives.

Now, allow your love to cover the entire earth. Taking a long, deep breath in, you then exhale and expand your love throughout the entire universe. A smile spreads across your face. Your heart has so much love to give that it can encompass all of time and space.

Now, see this expanded love as a net. It is now time for you to receive and slowly fold it in, like a blanket, bringing all of the love that you sent out back into you. Bring all that love back into your heart.

Your open heart has the power to heal the world.

Director's Notes

- ✺ To truly work with the three Universal Laws, be in a state of gratitude instead of a state of wanting and needing.

- ✺ Remembering what you're grateful for each evening is a powerful way to fall asleep.

- ✺ Call in more abundance by giving your time generously to others in acts both small and large.

- ✺ When you find yourself irritated by situations, people, or events, find something to be grateful for at that very moment.

Soulwork: Week IV

- ✹ Do a DreamStorm!

- ✹ Write How, What, and When action steps for each of your six intention cards. Do one step each day for the next 18 days.

- ✹ Identify three things that no longer serve you, and let go of them through a ritual.

- ✹ List five things you're grateful for each night.

- ✹ Do one selfless thing for someone each day.

- ✹ Continue your meditation and manifestation routine from Week III for the next seven days.

Week IV: Daily Meditation and Manifestation Routine

This is the written Week IV daily meditation practice, which is the same as Week III. You may want to have someone read it to you, or you may record it yourself. You can also download a free MP3 version from my website at **www.thecenterofgrace.com/meditation**.

Begin by using the Five-Senses Check-In to create a state of balance, clarity, and focus.

First, evoke the sense of sight. Look around the room. Notice the colors and textures. Move your eyes from object to object. If you notice a thought about the past or the future, simply move your gaze to the next object in the room. Notice anything in the room that you've never noticed before. What do you see?

Now, close your eyes and evoke the sense of smell. Breathe in deeply. Notice if you smell anything specific in the room. It could be something you cooked earlier, the scent of a candle, or a breeze coming through the window.

Next, evoke the sense of sound. Notice sounds inside the room. Then notice sounds coming from outside. Try listening with just your right ear and then your left.

Now, evoke the sense of touch. Notice how your feet feel on the floor. Then notice how your clothing feels on your body and how the air feels on your cheek.

Finally, evoke the sense of taste. Gently glide your tongue along the top of your teeth, and swallow.

Now just be.

Open your eyes and return to the room. Be here now.

Next, begin the manifestation portion of your daily routine. Have your six affirmation cards and your six intention cards ready. Start with affirmations. Read each card either aloud or silently to yourself. As you read, lift your heart and infuse yourself with confidence and knowing. Now do the same with your intentions, also reading them silently or aloud. As you read each card, again lift your heart and infuse yourself with confidence and knowing.

Close your eyes and imagine your intentions becoming reality. Envision your future-life script. As you visualize each of your scripted scenes, allow the music to move and assist you in matching your energetic frequency with the emotions connected to your manifestation.

Evoke all five senses until the movie feels real and true. Remember, you are the director of your destiny and the creator of your dreams. See it happening. Feel it becoming reality.

You are powerful beyond measure. This is your life and your movie. You get to decide how it ends.

Your work is done. Your intentions have been set. Commune in silence.

Begin your ten-minute meditation session by taking in three long, deep breaths. Straighten your spine and rest your hands lightly on your thighs.

Begin to follow your breath in and out. When a thought comes in, simply notice it. Do not label it as <u>good</u> or <u>bad</u>. Just say <u>Thinking</u> and return to your breath. You may want to use a mantra as you meditate. Say <u>in</u> on the inhalation and <u>out</u> on the exhalation. Or try <u>here</u> on the in breath and <u>now</u> on the out breath.

(Sit quietly for ten minutes of silent meditation.)

You have now completed your daily meditation and manifestation routine.

Now you have all nine practices. If you've finished the course, bravo! If not, remember that each day is an opportunity for a fresh start. You can always begin the course all over again.

I suggest trying all of the exercises in sequential order. Then, if necessary, reread the book for clarity. Many of my students keep coming back again and again.

This course is also available as a free four-week webinar when you become a member of The Circle of Grace. Please visit my website at **www.thecenterofgrace.com/membership** for more information on The Center of Grace Transformational Life School. I've created The Circle of Grace to help my students stay motivated and on track long after they've completed my course.

These practices and routines are a suggested way of doing things. Feel free—and even empowered—to alter anything and make them your own. You may prefer to meditate in the morning, journal in the afternoon, and read your intentions in the evening. All that really matters is taking the time, each day, to communicate with Source. Send out your intentions with powerful thoughts, beliefs, and emotions. Just be sure to put forth the effort to practice something every day.

The more attention you give to this work, the more results you'll see. This work extends far beyond just four weeks. These are lifetime practices to which you can continually return, as they're designed for you to cultivate self-mastery.

Remember, you are powerful beyond all measure. This is your life; this is your movie. You get to decide how it all ends.

Now go. Direct your destiny. Become the writer, producer, and director of your dreams.

In love and service,
Jennifer Grace

A DAILY ROUTINE
FOR MANIFESTING
YOUR DESTINY

This is most effective when you do it at the same time each day. Find a space in your home. Consider setting up a pillow and a small, low table with a candle.

This entire routine should only take 15 minutes.

Step 1: Be Present—The Five-Senses Check-In

Sit in the area that you have created for this daily ritual. Be present for a minute.

Slowly, one by one, check in with your senses. First, invoke the sense of sight by looking at the room. Notice all the colors and textures around you. If a thought comes in, simply notice it and move your gaze to the next object.

Now close your eyes and breathe deeply, invoking the sense of smell. Breathe in the air and notice whether you smell food, perfume, or the air itself.

Next, invoke the sense of sound. Listen to what sounds are coming from inside the room. Now listen for sounds coming from outside the room.

Then, invoke the sense of taste. Gently run your tongue along your teeth, and swallow.

Finally, invoke the sense of touch. Notice the way your clothing feels on your skin and the way the air feels on your cheek.

Then sit quietly and just be.

Step 2: Vocalize Your Daily Affirmations and Powerful Intentions

Say two things about yourself aloud that are currently the truth, such as your name and your place of birth. Then, either silently or aloud, read your six affirmations, followed by your six intentions. Make sure that you're not overly attached to these intentions, and trust that Source will work everything in the direction of your benefit.

Step 3: Heighten Your Emotional State

Each day, choose one future-life script to visualize in your mind movie. Play the soundtrack that goes with it to heighten your emotional state. Or, access a memory using the tool of substitution. Access a genuine past emotion relevant to this particular future scene. Imagine that you're living out this intention. See it and believe it. Above all, feel it.

Step 4: Perform a Sitting Meditation

Settle into a position to meditate. Set a timer for ten minutes. Close your eyes, straighten your spine, and sit up tall. Begin to follow your breath. Silently say *Om* to yourself on the inhalation and *Ah* on the exhalation. Repeat. Whenever a thought comes into your mind, simply notice it and go back to your breathing.

Step 5: Do a Gratitude Practice

Reflect on your day each evening and list in your journal five things for which you are grateful. Reread the list, feeling gratitude as you do so.

Step 6: Do a Generosity Practice

Perform an act of kindness, large or small, each day.

A PROFILE IN DIRECTING YOUR DESTINY

I creatively wrote this profile based on a true account of one of my students. Some of the minor details have been changed. My intention in including this profile is to help you see how all of the tools in this book can beautifully work together:

Maxie awoke from a restful night's sleep. She set her timer for five minutes, picked up her journal, and began to write. Along the way, she never lifted her pen from her paper:

> I'm a little tired but excited. Today I get to present my new clothing line to the investors. I know they will love it and give me all the money I need to manufacture this beautiful line of organic, eco-friendly clothing. I am so happy and confident that my Committee has quieted down and allowed me to have the courage to ask a group of people I have never met for $150,000. Today is my day. They will say yes . . .

After finishing her freedom writing, Maxie made her way to the kitchen to make tea. She had just painted the kitchen bright yellow. It set the tone for her day, as did her morning ritual, which she had come to love.

As her tea steeped, Maxie walked into her home office. She lit a candle at her meditation station. Sitting down on the large,

153

comfortable pillow she had found at the thrift store, she leaned over to smell the daisies that were in a vase by the window.

She took in three long, deep breaths and began her Five-Senses Check-In.

First, she invoked the sense of sight. She looked around at every object in the room. When a thought came into her head, she simply shifted her gaze and looked at the next object.

Then, she closed her eyes. Invoking the sense of smell, she noticed the scent of vanilla and peach wafting from her teacup.

Next, she just listened. Maxie noticed the sounds coming from inside the room. There was the hum of her computer. As she switched her attention to sounds outside the room, she heard birds singing and cars passing by her home.

For taste, she gently ran her tongue across her teeth. As she swallowed, she noticed the taste of the morning's toothpaste still lingering.

Finally, she invoked the sense of touch. She noticed the air crossing her cheek and the warmth of the sun streaming through her window.

Then she began to breathe slowly.

Opening her eyes, Maxie felt calm. She was centered and grounded, and ready to start her daily meditation and manifestation routine.

She picked up 14 three-by-five-inch cards and began.

First, she read her biographical cards, in order to say two things that were already true.

"I am Maxie Halpern."

"I am from Austin, Texas."

Next, she read aloud her six affirmation cards:

- ❋ *I am a magnet for opportunity and success.*

- ❋ *Every cell in my body is beaming with energy and light.*

- ❋ *I believe I have the power to create my world.*

- ❋ *I create abundance when I tap into my greatest gifts and share them with others.*

- ❋ *I love and accept myself exactly as I am.*

- ❋ *I take time to organize my life.*

That certainly silenced my Itty-Bitty Shitty Committee, she thought to herself.

Then she read her six intentions aloud with power and conviction:

❋ *I feel so grateful that I am now a successful clothing designer.*

❋ *I feel overjoyed that major department stores are carrying my line.*

❋ *I feel elated that I am now in partnership with conscious investors who want to make a difference and are funding my eco-clothing line.*

❋ *I feel blissed out that I am in a healthy love relationship.*

She laughed as she read the fourth intention and grabbed her pen. She wrote "Victory" across the card. It had now been two months, and her relationship with Jack was successful, healthy, and loving.

❋ *I feel at peace now that I am financially responsible.*

❋ *I feel proud that I am now in great shape and practicing yoga and meditation every day.*

She laughed again and wrote "Victory" across the sixth card, too. With two of her intentions accomplished, she made a note to create two new ones later that evening.

Now she began her manifestation practice.

Maxie switched on her music player, put on her headset, and began listening to "Good Life" by OneRepublic. Before pressing play, though, she read the future-life script she had written. It was designed to specifically work in partnership with conscious investors:

Future-Life Script Scene

Intention: I feel elated that I am now in partnership with conscious investors who want to make a difference and are funding my eco-clothing line.

Magic what if: What if I were to meet a group of people with the money to back my entire line?

Location: New York City

Wardrobe: Cream-colored, tailored suit and chocolate-brown heels with matching clutch handbag

Season: Fall

Time of day: 11:00 A.M.

Set: Boardroom

Props: Water glasses, coffee cups, notepads

Aromas: Coffee

Sounds: Ticking of clock on the boardroom wall

Soundtrack: "Good Life"

Emotional state: Elation!

Scene: I walk into the investors' boardroom looking well put together and wearing the eco-business suit I designed myself.

After reading the scene, Maxie suddenly became nervous. Later that day, she would have the opportunity to turn this script into reality. The opportunity first arose during a recent day at her office, where she worked as a dental receptionist. A patient had commented on her dress, admiring the design. She had smiled and explained that it was actually her own.

He raised his eyebrows and asked about the material. Maxie explained that it was from natural fibers that were grown without pesticides or other toxic materials. The process, she explained, helped to preserve the health of humans and the environment.

He smiled. "What else do you design?"

She told him about her signature Corporate Zen line, which includes business suits for both men and women.

He raised his eyebrows again. "Today may be your lucky day," he said.

He handed her his business card. His name was Dan Portman, and his company was looking to expand into environmentally friendly businesses.

"This just might be the answer," he said.

He told her to call and set up a meeting with his board. She looked at the address: Madison Avenue. Smiling from ear to ear, she promised to call the next day.

Having been in New York for two years, and having been rejected again and again by fashion houses, Maxie could barely believe that a potential investor had literally walked right into her life.

Maxie loathed her job as a receptionist. Even though she had refused to allow it to get her down, it was sometimes a challenge to be grateful for the job. But now, because of it, she had met Dan. It was something she never thought would happen.

That's what not being attached to the outcome probably looks like, she thought to herself. She certainly never had imagined that a funder for her clothing line would walk through the door of a dentist's office!

Maxie smiled at the memory. She took a few more breaths to calm her nerves. The meeting had been two weeks ago, and today she would present her line to Dan's board.

It was essential that today, of all days, she manifest with every ounce of energy and send a positive message to Source.

Unfortunately, she currently felt more freaked out than elated.

She decided to use the substitution tool to recall a time when she was filled with elation.

Maxie thought back to her time on the high school swim team when she'd won an award for having the fastest time in the butterfly stroke. She'd broken the school record and won the championship for her team. As she journeyed back to that day, she filled in the details.

Once she conjured up the elation, she felt it course through every bone in her body. Then she pressed Play and let "Good Life" fill her ears. It was the soundtrack of her future-life script.

Maxie shifted from the past to the future. She saw herself confidently walking into the boardroom. Dan was smiling. She imagined giving them an incredible presentation. The realness of the meeting filled her, along with the excitement of securing funding.

In her mind's eye, she saw everyone nodding yes.

When the song ended, she took her earplugs out. Then, she set her meditation timer for ten minutes and sat in silence.

Her intentions were set. She had communicated with Source using her positive thoughts, beliefs, and emotions. Now there was nothing left to do except . . . be.

Maxie sat up on her pillow and imagined a golden string pulling her toward the sky. She took long, slow breaths. On her inhalations, she said, *Here.* On her exhalations, she said, *Now.*

After just a few moments, she felt Source move through her. She also felt the connection of all that is and the power of her own personal energy.

The timer went off. Maxie began her day.

The taxi let her out in front of Dan's impressive building on Madison Avenue. She smiled at herself. She was grateful that her boss, Dr. Roberts, had given her the day off.

Her heart began beating faster as she walked into the building.

Suddenly, someone on her Itty-Bitty Shitty Committee said, *You're a fool. You've never designed a professional line in your life. What makes you think someone will just hand you $150,000?*

This voice was joined by that of another member of the Committee. *That's right,* this one said. *You have absolutely no experience. These people will just laugh at you. You should turn around and go home.*

As she got on the elevator, Maxie took out her invisible remote, pointed it at them, and pressed Mute.

You've been designing clothes since you were six years old, she reminded herself. *You've got this, girl! Feel the fear, but do it anyway.*

She smiled, recognizing her voice of wisdom. Then she got off the elevator and walked confidently down the hall.

The meeting went flawlessly. She really felt that they loved the design and concept of her line. When she said she needed $150,000 to manufacture the first run, no one blinked an eye.

Dan promised to call her the next day with an answer.

She couldn't wipe the smile off her face during the elevator ride back down. Her future-life script had been manifested. In fact, the boardroom in which she had presented looked incredibly similar to the one in her mind movie. It was almost uncanny!

Maxie could have written any future-life script about any investor. She could have envisioned meeting a woman who owned a yoga studio and wanted to hold a meeting there. Instead, she had scripted a meeting in a corporate boardroom. And that is exactly what had manifested.

All of Maxie's hard work was coming to fruition. She had made her How, What, and When action plans and had been doing at least three action steps each week. She stayed with her daily manifestation and meditation routine. Each night, she was grateful for a good job and wonderful friends. She'd even tried to do a selfless act of kindness each day.

She also knew that even if Dan called the next day with bad news, Source would eventually lead her to a perfect yes.

She returned home and lay down on her couch. She allowed herself to relax after such a stimulating morning. She looked around her apartment and admired her surroundings.

Then, her mind started to wander toward the future, worrying about Dan's call the next day. She gently guided her thoughts back to the present. She took in a few deep breaths and continued to look around the room.

Then, her phone alarm sounded. It was her daily reminder to "Be. Here. Now." She smiled, realizing that she was doing just that.

Maxie liked the movie she had created for herself. She was now sitting in the director's chair. Her right-hand man, Will, had helped get all of her designs together for that morning's presentation. Grace, her left-hand woman, had orchestrated the divine encounter with Dan. Everything was in synchronicity.

That night, her new love, Jack, was taking her out for a romantic dinner. They could celebrate her first big meeting with a real investor. Whether the funding came through or not, she could be proud of making it this far. She smiled at this wonderful new movie that she was starring in.

It was a great movie. She had, after all, written it herself.

ACKNOWLEDGMENTS

Thanks to Amanda and Joseph Safina, who have been instrumental in supporting me through this entire process and leading me to the serendipitous moment of Grace that allowed this book to manifest.

Thanks to Serena Dyer and Wayne Dyer for guiding me in the right direction.

Thanks to my mom and dad, Donna Jenson and George DeQuattro, for raising me with unconditional love, support, and empowerment; and to their partners, Charles Holmes and Angela DeQuattro, for being the most amazing stepparents ever. Thanks also to my Aunt Jeanne for the wisdom she always shares with me.

Thanks to my Dream Team, without whose presence this book would not be possible: Audrey Denson, my BFF and creative art director, whose work is always fabulous and flawless; and my editors, Neil Gordon and Steve Ralls, who took my words to a whole different stratosphere—you both rock! Thanks also to my social-media guru, Franky Arriola, and my PR maven, Jenny Lee Molina, for getting the word out in a big way.

Thanks to my agent, Estella Arias; my website developer, Debbie Duke; and my right-hand woman, Grace Delanoy, for being there every step of the way.

Thanks to my three mentors: Dr. Jessica Gurvit, Julia Romaine, and Christan Hummel, who helped me lay down an unshakable foundation for my work to stand upon.

Thanks to Alyson Calagna (Bodhi) for cheering me on with boundless love and support in the beginning.

Thanks to John Paul for giving me unconditional love and endless motivation as I crossed the finish line with this book.

Thanks to Thea Sommer, who gave me the push I needed to become the coach I am today.

Thanks to Mina Gough, Amanda Hale De Jesus, and everyone at The Standard Spa, Miami Beach, who have been an amazing support team.

Thanks to my oceanfront-home angels, Lisa Dei Jacobs and Linda Carol, for providing me their homes to write in; the beautiful backdrops were certainly inspirational.

Thanks to my friends and confidants who always call me out when I need them to and always keep me laughing and smiling. I shall list your names in alphabetical order, because I love you all equally: Zuseth Amador, Filiz Bakir, Jane Bolin, Alison Burgos, Ashley Carroll, Darren Cefalu, Jessica Concepcion, Jane Dagmi, Michelle Gaber, Gwen Gaydos, Luciana Genova, Seth and Lisa Grossman, Pamela Jones, Jayne Mills, Deanna Padgett, Luciana Pavan, Joanna Popper, Maria Pulice, Sari Rauch, and Ash Ruiz.

Thanks to Arianna Goldman for being an incredible lawyer and an amazing friend.

Thanks to the entire Hay House family, which I feel proud to now be a part of.

And thanks to Nicole, my very own guardian angel, for always looking out.

ABOUT THE AUTHOR

Jennifer Grace received a B.A. in communications from the University of Arizona. She spent eight years on Wall Street in investment banking, and then crossed over into the creative world and became a SAG actress, filmmaker, and screenwriter. In the last seven years, she has blended her business knowledge and creative expertise to become an executive dream producer, which gives her and her Dream Team the opportunity to help others discover their personal dreams and then launch them into reality. She is trained and certified in Creativity in Business, the famed Stanford University personal transformation postgraduate course, which she teaches locally at her Transformational Life School at The Center of Grace. She is currently leading retreats all over the world, hosting webinars, and loving being a mom to her son, Cole Sebastian, who frequently shows up at her classes as a guest teacher!

Websites: **www.jennifergrace.com** and **www.thecenterofgrace .com**

We hope you enjoyed this Hay House book. If you'd like to receive our online catalog featuring additional information on Hay House books and products, or if you'd like to find out more about the Hay Foundation, please contact:

Hay House, Inc., P.O. Box 5100, Carlsbad, CA 92018-5100
(760) 431-7695 or (800) 654-5126
(760) 431-6948 (fax) or (800) 650-5115 (fax)
www.hayhouse.com® • **www.hayfoundation.org**

Published and distributed in Australia by: Hay House Australia Pty. Ltd.,
18/36 Ralph St., Alexandria NSW 2015 • *Phone:* 612-9669-4299
Fax: 612-9669-4144 • www.hayhouse.com.au

Published and distributed in the United Kingdom by: Hay House UK, Ltd.,
Astley House, 33 Notting Hill Gate, London W11 3JQ
Phone: 44-20-3675-2450 • *Fax:* 44-20-3675-2451 • www.hayhouse.co.uk

Published and distributed in the Republic of South Africa by: Hay House SA (Pty),
Ltd., P.O. Box 990, Witkoppen 2068 • *Phone/Fax:* 27-11-467-8904
www.hayhouse.co.za

Published in India by: Hay House Publishers India, Muskaan Complex, Plot No. 3,
B-2, Vasant Kunj, New Delhi 110 070 • *Phone:* 91-11-4176-1620
Fax: 91-11-4176-1630 • www.hayhouse.co.in

Distributed in Canada by: Raincoast, 9050 Shaughnessy St., Vancouver, B.C. V6P 6E5
Phone: (604) 323-7100 • *Fax:* (604) 323-2600 • www.raincoast.com

Take Your Soul on a Vacation

Visit **www.HealYourLife.com®** to regroup, recharge,
and reconnect with your own magnificence.
Featuring blogs, mind-body-spirit news, and
life-changing wisdom from Louise Hay and friends.

Visit **www.HealYourLife.com** today!